Cou

L

South Downs - West
Hampshire

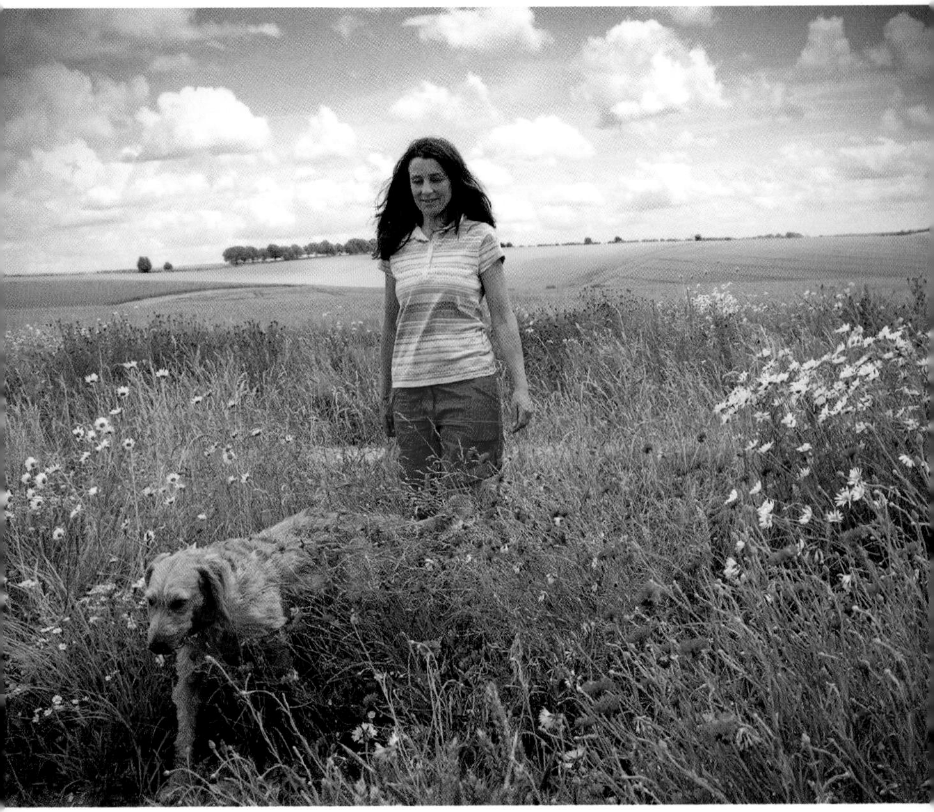

www.countrysidedogwalks.co.uk

First published in December 2015 by **Wet Nose Publishing Ltd**

All enquiries regarding sales telephone: 01824 704398
email cdw@wetnosepublishing.co.uk
www.countrysidedogwalks.co.uk
ISBN 978-0-9931923-0-2

 British Library Cataloguing-in-publication data.
A catalogue is available for this book from the British Library. Whilst every effort has been made to ensure that the information in this book is correct, the author or the publisher can accept no responsibility for errors, loss or injury however caused. Maps based upon out of copyright Ordnance Survey mapping.
Printed in Poland
www.lfbookservices.co.uk

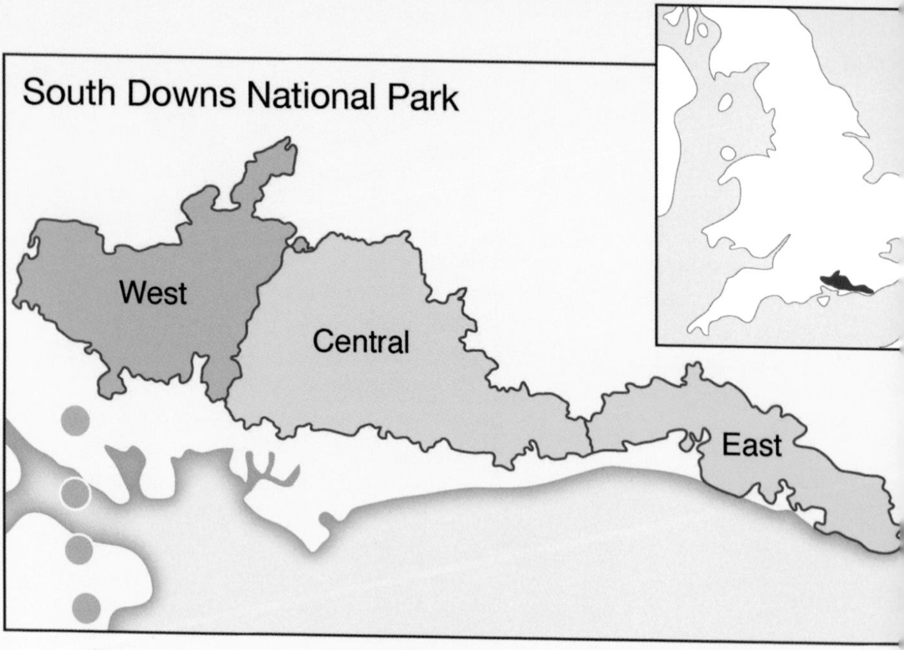

South Downs National Park

West

Central

East

South Downs - West

Alton

Bordon

Winchester

Petersfield

Havant

A31

A3

10
9
8
7
6
1
17
19
18
16
20
12
15
2
11
5
3
4
14
13

Contents

Introduction

The twenty walks included in this book are all designed so that you and your wet nosed friend have a really enjoyable time. Where there are stiles, they are specially designed with lift gates for dogs. At a quick glance there is information at the beginning of each walk to tell you what to expect and what you may need to take with you. The descriptive guides will also warn of any roads ahead or areas of livestock so that you can get your dog on the lead well in advance.

Dogs just love to explore new places. They really enjoy the new smells and carry themselves a little higher with the added excitement. Going to new places gets you and your dog out and about, meeting new people and their dogs. It is important to socialise dogs, as they will be more likely to act in a friendly manner towards other dogs as they gain confidence.

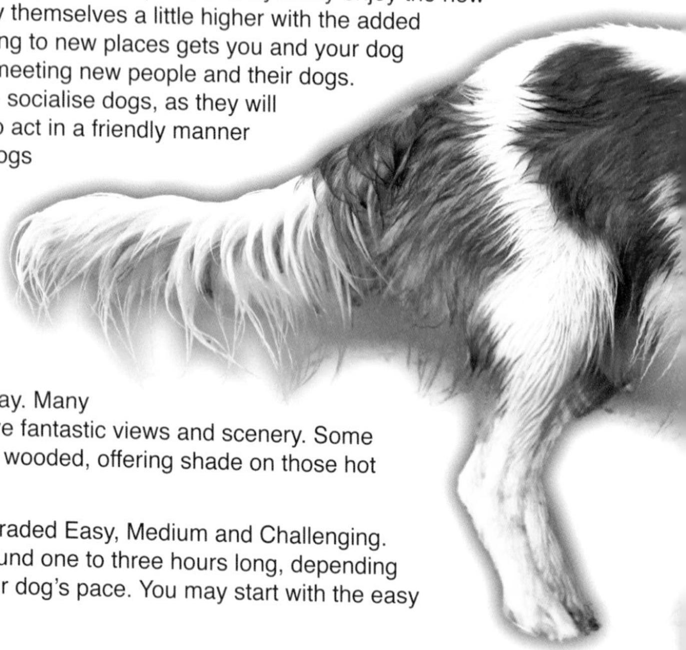

The stunning pictures in this book are just a taster of what you can see along the way. Many of the walks have fantastic views and scenery. Some of the walks are wooded, offering shade on those hot summer days.

The walks are graded Easy, Medium and Challenging. They are all around one to three hours long, depending on your and your dog's pace. You may start with the easy

ones and work up to the challenging walks depending on your and your dog's fitness. Different dog breeds and dog age must be taken into account when you decide which walks to do.

Different breeds of dog have different levels of fitness. For example, bulldogs can only do short walks whereas a border collie or a springer spaniel are extremely energetic and difficult to tire out. It is recommended that you do some research on the breed of dog that you own to get to know what sort of exercise that they require.

You may have a walk that you are happy doing with your dog every day, but this book will show you new areas to explore with a change of scenery and a chance to meet new people and their dogs. Dogs love new places to visit and you will see the change in them as they explore the new surroundings, taking in the new smells with delight. You will fulfil both your life and your dog's just by trying somewhere new.

Some of the walks include bridleways, so you may encounter horses and cyclists. It is important to put your dog on a lead if you see horses approach. It is always helpful to say hello to the riders as they near so that the horse realises that you are not a threat.

The South Downs National Park

The South Downs National Park was designated in April 2011. It covers 628 square miles from Winchester in the west to Eastbourne in the east. The area includes part of Hampshire and parts of East and West Sussex. Although newly recognised as a National Park, the fight for designation has been going on since the 1920s to protect the iconic landscape from threats such as development of industry and housing, ploughing up of the herb-rich chalk downland, which is important for many rare and specialist species, protection from deforestation of its vast and beautiful wooded hillsides, and destruction of heathlands. The latter supports all of our British reptiles, some of which are very rare. The South Downs Way (SDW) long distance path is 100 miles long and crosses the length of the National Park, following the chalk ridge through Sussex and part of Hampshire. Many of the circular walks in this book have included part of the SDW.

There are numerous quintessentially English villages throughout the National Park, with many thatched cottages. The unique flint and red brick buildings and walls and split rail fencing are authentic to the area and highlight exceptional craftsmanship, using locally sourced materials. The flint and chalk is visible in ploughed fields and can be seen clearly on eroded grass paths. It is used to surface many footpaths throughout the National Park. The timber for the fencing is sourced from the many sweet chestnut coppiced woods.

Ground Nesting Birds

Watch out for vulnerable ground nesting birds during 1st of March until the end of July. Dogs that stray off the main paths may disturb birds and chicks, possibly killing them or breaking eggs. Species to look out for are Sky larks, Meadow pipits, Curlew, Red and Black grouse, Snipe and Pheasants.

Some if not all of these birds are declining in numbers, due partly to their vulnerability when nesting. Dogs are a threat to them, even if treading on them unintentionally. Some other threats are foxes, badgers, stoats, weasels, birds of prey and crows.

Please help to protect these birds during the nesting season by keeping your dog on the paths when walking in open areas such as grassland, moors, heathland and scrub.

Rivers

Some dogs love water and will think nothing of plunging into the river. With the extreme weather conditions over the last few years, a river that may be safe for your dog to swim in can change in a matter of hours to become a swollen torrent that could wash your dog away. Please be careful when near rivers if there have been heavy periods of rain or if they look swollen or fast flowing. It is best to put your dogs on the lead, until you have assessed the situation.

Livestock

If you find that you need to cross a field with cattle or horses and they seem interested in you or your dog it is recommended within the Countryside Code to let your dog off the lead. Never try to get between livestock and your dog. Your dog will get out of a situation a lot more easily with speed than you can. It is usually only cattle with young calves that are a threat, or young heifers or bullocks that tend to get a little inquisitive. They will usually stop when they get close to you or your dog.

Most horses will come over for a fuss but a small proportion do have a problem with dogs. They may see them as a threat and will act to defend the herd. Horses that are out with a rider are completely different as they are not defending the herd, and as long as you keep a safe distance there should not be a problem.

Sheep are not a danger to you, but your dog can be a danger to them. Where sheep are grazing it is vital that you have your dog on a lead or under very close control. You will know your dog, but if you are unsure it is better to play safe and keep your dog on a lead. It is important always to have your dog on a lead when around lambs. Lambs have a higher pitched bleat and can be the size of a cat, and your dog may act differently amongst them.

Ticks

If you have been walking in areas where sheep graze you should check your dog for ticks. They must be removed as soon as possible. It is best to use tick tweezers, which are specially designed to remove the head and leg parts of the tick. Ticks can carry diseases and the longer they remain latched on to your dog the more the chance of spreading infections.

Forests

The forest walks in this book are a changing landscape, which makes them unique and interesting. Descriptions may change with time, for instance a path may be described as being in the shade of the forest, but as this is a worked forest a section could be clear felled at any time. Another change over the years could be where a view is described across a previously felled area. This could then be planted up and trees grown blocking the views. Paths may change but this is less likely. On rare occasions the Forestry Commission may temporarily close paths due to forest works but again this is even less likely on a weekend. Any changes to the path networks that may occur after the date of print will be updated on our website.

Does your dog fetch a stick?

Most dogs love sticks and will pick them up without any encouragement from their owners. Vets and dog trainers recommend that you should not throw sticks for dogs. They can cause nasty injuries, sometimes fatal as the stick can pierce the throat, or rebound off the ground and cause harm to your dog.

Please clean up after your dog

Always be prepared, having dog bags with you at all times. Once you have cleaned up after your dog, please keep the bag, until you see a bin. If there are no bins provided, then take it away with you to a roadside bin. Dog bags that are discarded on the paths or in the bushes are unpleasant and unsightly and will not degrade.

1. Liss Forest

Medium - 3.2 miles - 1hr 30min

This circular walk passes through fabulous heathland, with gorse scrub, silver birch and pine woodland. The tracks are well-made and undulating. There are views on some parts of the walk. One of the main tracks is a disused railway, which was put in to transport soldiers from Rogate to Jolly Drover in the Second World War. The site is owned by the MOD, and there may be army vehicles on the tracks at times. Your dog can find water in places. There may be livestock and during the nesting season keep your dog on the paths to protect ground-nesting birds. There may be gunfire heard on a rifle range in the distance, which may frighten some dogs.

How to get there – From Petersfield join the A3 in the direction of London and Guildford. Leave the A3 at the roundabout and follow the sign for Selborne (not Liss) on the B3003. Shortly after, follow the sign for Greatham Village and turn right. Turn next right, just after at the church. You will pass over the A3 and shortly after you will reach the car park on your left.

Grid Reference – SU 780292 **Postcode** - GU33 7BX

Parking – Free in the car park

Facilities – There are no facilities

You will need – Dog leads, dog bags

The Walk

❶ From the car park go through the gate beside the cattle grid, which is opposite the car park entrance. Continue on the wide path, and take a path on your right shortly after. Pass an interpretation panel on your left and continue through the woodland.

Ascend on the path. There is a sharp right bend where you will reach an open area of heathland on your left. Continue on the main surfaced track. Ignore any paths on your left and right. The track will ascend a little way. There are views just before the path bends to your left, if you look behind you.

Continue on the main surfaced track, below the power lines. Pass a small gate on your right and a vehicle gate just after. There is gorse and silver birch on your left and woodland on your right, with a barbed wire fence. The exposed soil here is sandy. The track is undulating and will continue for quite a distance. Ignore any paths on your left and right.

The track veers away from the fence line on your right a little, and will continue beside the gorse scrub on your left, with some silver birch and Scot's pine. You will pass a danger sign for deep water on your right. This is a ditch, where your dog can cool off in hot weather.

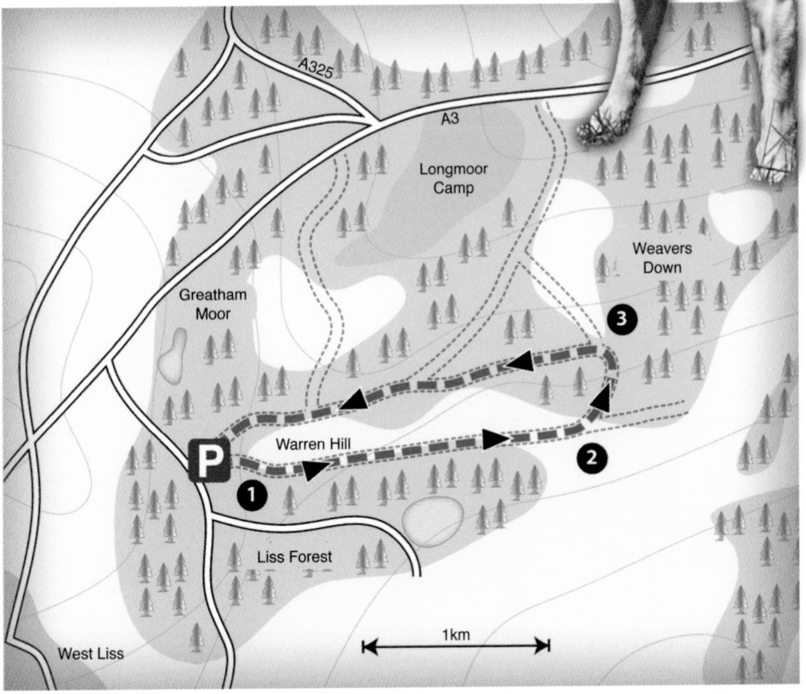

❷ After some distance the track bends sharply to your left, just as you reach the top of a hill. Continue on the track here, ignoring the grass track straight ahead. This track ascends gently through the middle of beautiful hilly heathland. There are gorse, pines and silver birch scattered throughout the area. On reaching a cross of tracks turn left. Continue between pine trees and you will soon descend. Continue on this track for some distance.

There are open pockets of heathland on your left and right, where the trees clear. You will have views ahead, across the heathland to trees in the far distance. The track will bend to your right. Continue on the track, ignoring a path on your left and right. As you continue you will turn another bend to your right. You will then meet another track. ❸ Turn left on this track, which was once a railway in the Second World War.

The trees are quite dense here. Continue on the main track, ignoring any paths on your left and right. You will pass a post and rail fence on your left and right. Your dog may find water here, beside the path, depending on how much rainfall there has been. As you continue there is a pond on your right (soon after passing the second path on your right), below the bank. Your dog can cool off here. Continue on this track, where you will see the gate to the car park ahead soon after.

2. Petersfield Heath

Easy - 1.16 miles - 1hr

This is a delightful short circular walk. You will pass through meadows, with blocks of mixed deciduous woodland. In the summer months many butterflies flutter amongst the wild flowers, and you may hear skylarks. Pass beside Petersfield Cricket Pitch, and continue ambling through the wide meadows with scattered trees. You will reach a lake, where your dog can have a dip. Please keep your dog on the paths from April until end of July, because there may be ground nesting birds. There are no roads or livestock on this walk.

How to get there – Petersfield Heath can be found near to the centre of Petersfield. Follow the brown sign for Heath Pond and Parking, on the B2146. Park in the main car park, not the lay-by.

Grid Reference – SU 754225
Postcode – GU31 4LD

Parking – Free

Facilities – There are no facilities

You will need – Dog lead, dog bags

The Walk

❶ From the car park entrance, with your back to the road, take the path on the right hand side of the car park, midway along. Take the wider path between the trees. On reaching the meadow, take the path on your right. Pass a bench on your right. Keep your dog under close control, as there is a road ahead with no boundary fences. The path crosses the meadow, heading towards the trees. In the summer months there are lots of butterflies.

Just before reaching the trees, another path will join the path which you are on from your left. You will reach the trees, and then the path bends to the left, passing beneath the tree canopy. Continue on the path with the trees on your left, at the edge of the meadow. The road is beyond the trees on your right. When you reach the end of the trees on your left, continue straight ahead, crossing through the meadow. Cross another path close to the edge of the meadow, and continue straight ahead.

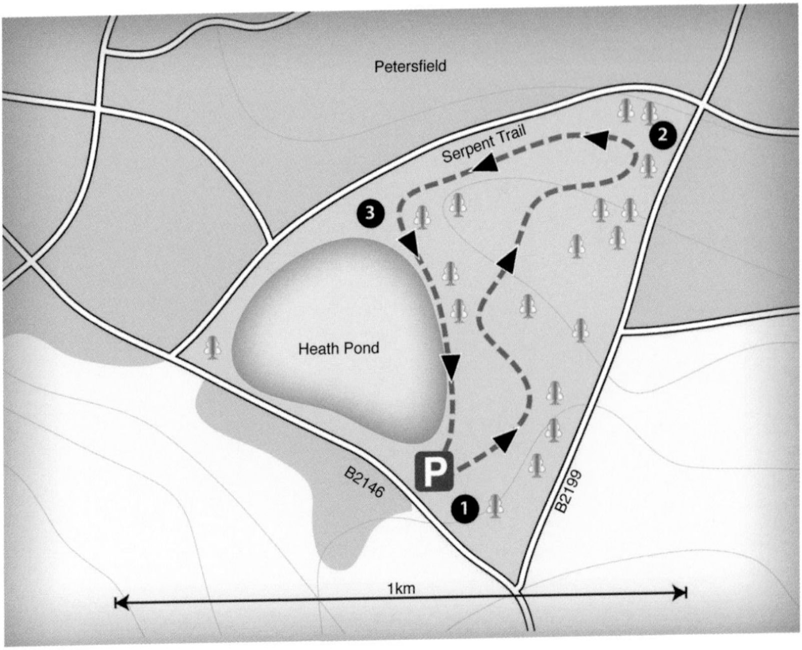

Cross a footbridge over a ditch, where dogs can cool off in hot weather. There are woods on your left, and the meadow on your right. Continue on the wide path, ignoring a narrow path on your right, and enter into the mixed broadleaved woodland. Take the next path on your right soon after. Take a narrow path on your right, and soon you will reach another path. Turn left on this path.

Keep your dog under close control, as you will soon reach a cricket pitch. The road is still on your right. On reaching the pitch, put your dog on a lead or under close control and turn right. Walk on the edge of the pitch, with trees and scrub on your right. Continue beside a split rail fence on your left. You will reach a surfaced path. Turn left on this path, and continue on the edge of the pitch.

After passing the cricket pitch, take a path on your left, ❷ beside a bank on your left. Continue on the wider path, through the middle of the meadow. You now leave the road behind. Cross another path and continue straight ahead. Continue straight ahead through the middle of the meadow, passing 'The Little School' on your far right. Pass a block of trees on your left, and continue towards houses on your right and ahead.

Continue on the worn sandy path, ignoring the path on your left. The meadow on your right is cut here for recreation purposes. Follow the path as it bends to your left. You will then reach the lake. On reaching the lake path, turn left. ❸

Continue on this path beside the lake. There are mixed broadleaved trees on your left, and willow on your right. You will see lots of wildfowl on the banks, and on the water. Keep close control of your dog, as there may be territorial swans or chicks in spring and early summer. You will pass several benches on your left.

Ignore any paths on your left and look out for black iron fencing on your left. On reaching the fencing put your dog on a lead or under very close control, as there is a busy road ahead. You will soon see the car park on the left, as you pass the notice board.

3. Queen Elizabeth Park Med - 3.5 miles - 2hr 30min

This circular walk is predominantly within the Queen Elizabeth forest, which has wide, well-made paths, therefore you will be free from livestock for the best part, however there may be deer in the area. There are some views after an ascent, which show the beauty of the surrounding area. Cyclists and horse riders share the paths. Near the end of the walk you will cross through farmland, where sheep or cattle may be grazing.

How to get there – From Petersfield, take the B2070. Follow the sign for Plymouth and the A3. After crossing the railway bridge turn left at the roundabout, and follow the sign for Buriton. At the road junction beside The Maple Inn, turn right onto Kiln Lane. You will see Halls Hill car park on your right, a little further along the road. The postcode will take you to The Maple Inn.

Grid Reference – SU 733197
Nearest Postcode – GU31 5SW

Parking – Free in Forestry Commission car park (Halls Hill)

Facilities – There are no facilities, but there are picnic benches along the way.

You will need – Dog leads, dog bags and water for your dog.

The Walk

❶ From the car park take the track on the opposite side of the entrance, which is part of the South Downs Way (SDW) long distance footpath. Pass beside the notice board and a vehicle barrier. There are trees on your right, and fields on your left, which has a barbed wire fence. The path becomes quite steep, with trees on both sides, offering shade in places. Beware of cyclists passing across your track. Keep your dog under close control.

You will pass a chalk sculpture of a sheep and a bench on your left, where you can see beautiful views across miles of countryside with hills beyond. The path is level now. Ignore a path on your right, which ascends into the woods. The path now descends. Another wide track joins the track which you are on from your right. Here you will see another bench with a view on your left. You will now descend a little steeper. Ignore a path on your left and continue to descend through mixed broadleaved woodland. The gradient will lessen now.

After a while you will pass a barbecue and picnic area on your left, and a path on your right. Continue straight ahead. After some

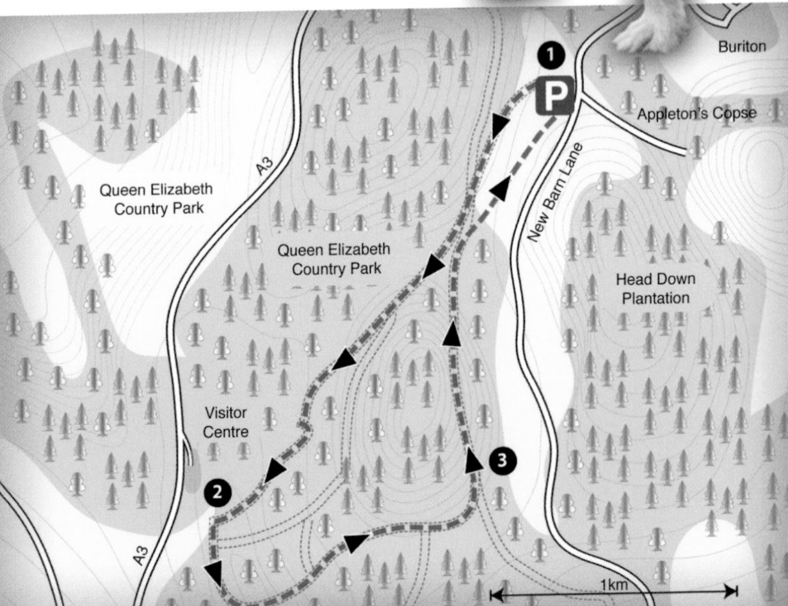

distance, when you see a vehicle barrier, call your dogs close. Pass beside the vehicle barrier and interpretation panel to reach a car park on your left and a picnic area. Put your dog on a lead, and on reaching the road turn left. ❷ Just as you pass a bend in the road, take the path on your left, signed Hangers Way and SDW. You will now enter back into the woods.

The road continues parallel with the path that you are on, so keep your dog under close control or on a lead. You will pass another car park on your right. Continue straight ahead, passing a waymarker on your right. Turn left on meeting another track and ascend, you have now left the SDW. Ignore a path, indicated by a fingerpost on your right. Ignore another path on your right, just after and continue on the wide track which veers to your left. Follow the small way-marker signed for Shipwrights Way and Staunton Way.

Ascend on the path, and after the ascent ignore a path on your right and continue. Immediately after you will pass another chalk sculpture on your right. The track levels off here. There are coniferous trees on your left.

Ignore a path on your left a little further along. As you continue, there are coniferous trees on both sides of the track and you will begin to ascend.

A track crosses the track which you are on. There is a forest clearing on your right, which enables you to see a view, but only briefly. There are now broadleaved woods once again. Pass a narrow path on your left, and just after, pass paths on your left and right. Soon after you will pass a turning area for forestry vehicles on your left, and then just after this, pass paths on your left and right.

The track now descends. Ignore a path on your right and then immediately after, take the path on your left, ❸ both paths are indicated by a fingerpost on your right. The path ascends into the woods. Ignore a path on your left and right and shortly after you will reach level ground. A little further on, the path descends gently, cutting across the sloped beech woodland. Ignore a path on your left, which is indicated by a fingerpost for SDW (Riders). Almost immediately after, ignore paths on your right and left. Continue straight ahead, and take the next path on your right, where you will see a fingerpost signed for Hanger Way and Staunton Way.

This path is narrow and you descend between young mixed broadleaved trees. You will reach a kissing gate. Put your dog on a lead or under close control here. Pass through the kissing gate into pasture, where you may encounter livestock. There may be a water trough here, where thirsty dogs can get a drink. Continue straight ahead at the top edge of the field. There is a narrow woodland strip on your left, and a house below on your right.

On reaching the end of the field, pass through another kissing gate and cross through the middle of the field, veering slightly to your right to begin with. Head for the gate, just before the corner of the field, following the worn grass track. Pass through the kissing gate, and cross another shorter path across a field. You will reach another kissing gate, which leads into the car park.

4. Queen Elizabeth VC

Med - 1.9 miles - 1hr 30min

This circular walk is within the forest, and is mostly on wide well-made paths. There are no steep ascents, and the paths are mostly undulating. You will pass an area where you will have views across the hilly countryside. There are no roads or livestock; however there may be deer in the area.

How to get there – From Petersfield, join the A3 following the sign for Portsmouth. Turn off the A3 when you see the brown sign for Queen Elizabeth Country Park, which is located just off the A3. Follow the brown signs until reaching the car park.

Grid reference – SU 718185
Postcode – P08 0QE

Parking – Pay and display

Facilities – There is a visitor centre, café and toilets

You will need – Dog lead, dog bags and water for your dog

The Walk

❶ From the entrance to the visitor centre, with your back to the door, take a path ahead and right, where you will see a giant fingerpost. Take the first footpath on your right, signed Short Woodland Trail on the South Downs Way (SDW) long distance footpath. Keep your dog under close control or on a lead to begin with, as there are further car parking areas and a road ahead.

Pass a picnic area behind the visitor centre, and then a pond on your right. Pass a fenced play area on your left. You will see a BBQ and picnic area on your right. On reaching a road, cross it and turn left, and almost immediately right. Pass beside a vehicle barrier and ascend the path. ❷ Turn right, and follow the green footprints for quite some time. Your dog is safe from roads here.

Ignore a path on your right and then ignore a track on your left. You will have a forest on your left and a wire fence on your right with pasture beyond it. Ignore another path on your left and continue on the path, descending gently. Ignore a path on your right and continue to descend.

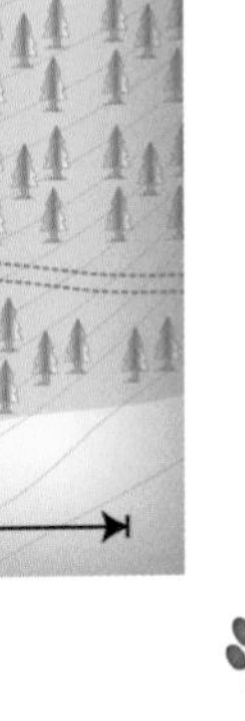

You will ascend a little way, and then reach level ground. Pass a bench on your right, where you will see views across the countryside, with a windmill in the distance. You will descend again, and pass another bench on your right. Ignore a path on your left, which is indicated by the green footprint way-markers. Continue straight ahead, and ascend once again on the track.

Stay on the track, following a sharp bend on your left, ❸ ignoring a path ahead and to your right. The track ascends, and after a short distance, ❹ take a path on your left (not the path on your right, which is indicated by a red footprint). Descend through a forest clearing. As you reach the trees the path bends to your left. There are broadleaved trees on your left, and coniferous trees on your right.

The path narrows where the immediate woods are dominated by silver birch, with coniferous trees beyond. Ignore a path on your right. A little further along oak trees dominate. On reaching another track, turn right. You will now follow the green footprint way-markers again.

On reaching another track turn left. Keep your dog under close control and descend back to the road. Cross the road and turn right. Follow this path, where you will retrace your steps back to the visitor centre.

5. Butser Hill

Easy - 1 miles - 1hr

This wonderful walk is packed with views as you walk amongst the meadows on the chalk hill. It is the highest point of the chalk ridge within the South Downs, and the second highest point within the National Park. You will reach this point with very little effort, as the car park is located on the top. In the summer months you will see many butterflies enjoying the wild flowers. You may also hear the skylarks calling. There are ground-nesting birds during the nesting season, so it would be better to keep your dog on a lead or under close control and on the paths. At times there may be livestock grazing. There are no roads.

How to get there – From Petersfield, join the A3 following the sign for Portsmouth. Turn off when you see the sign for Butser Hill and Hambledon. Turn right at the roundabout, following the sign for London and Petersfield. Shortly after turn left, and follow the signs for Butser Hill, where you will reach the car park.

Grid Reference – SU 711200

Parking – Pay and display

Facilities – There are toilets and a snack bar, but opening times are seasonal

You will need – Dog lead, dog bags and water for your dog

The Walk

❶ From the car park, continue to the furthest end of the middle row of bays. Take the path, which will meet with a quiet access road. Ascend and on your left you will reach a kiosk and toilets with a coned roof. Pass the kiosk and a disabled parking bay. Go through the gate ahead. Turn immediately left on a worn grass path. There is a block of hawthorn on your left and a meadow on your right.

You will have amazing views on your left. ❷ Continue passed a gate on your left. Ignore another gate in the corner of the meadow and turn right, and follow beside the fence on your left. Stay on the worn grass path. Where the fence line turns a corner continue straight ahead through the middle of the meadow. On reaching beside the stock fence once again, turn left. Stay beside the stock fence on the worn path. The fence ends where you continue straight ahead.

The views on your left extend across beautiful hilly countryside. You will reach another stock fence on your right. Ignore the path on your left and continue passed the enclosure on your right, and then turn right. Follow the grass path through the meadow, passing some hawthorn trees on your left.

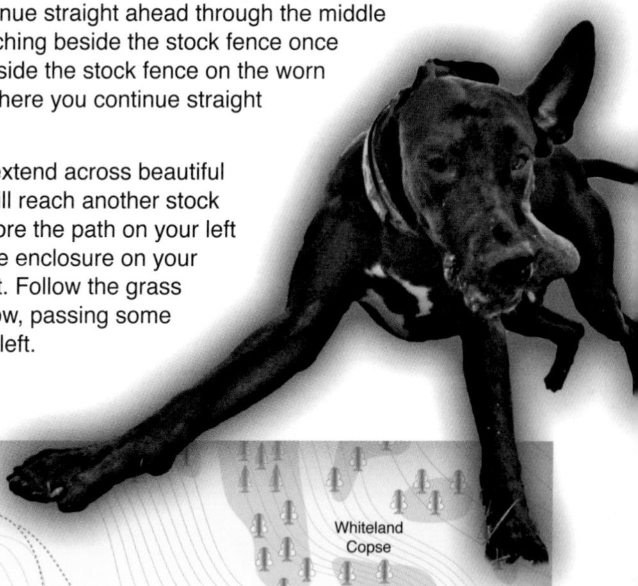

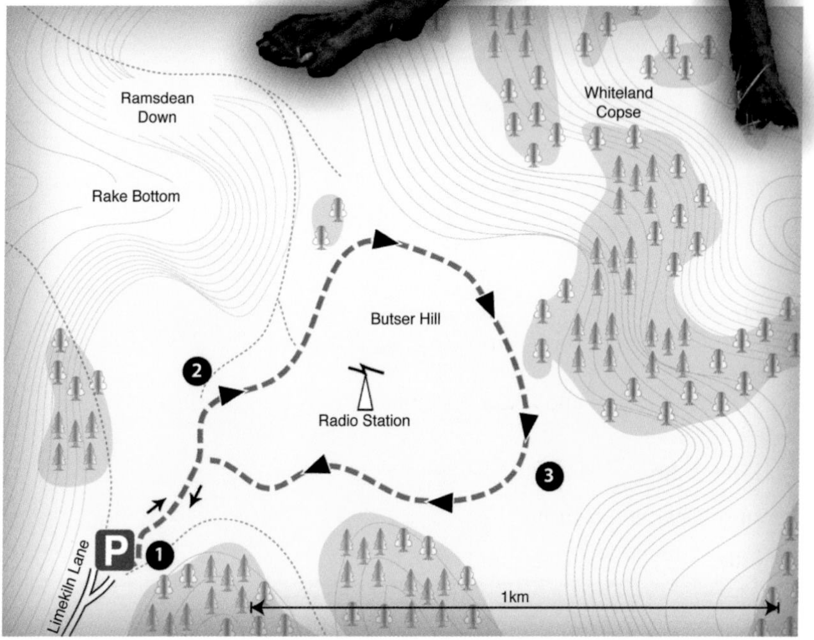

Ignore a path on your right and continue straight ahead, soon after ignore a path on your left and right. Pass a trig point on your far right. ❸ As you continue ignore another path on your left and right. You will turn a bend, where another path joins the path which you are on from your left.

You now have new views, across the beautiful countryside to the sea and the Isle of White. Continue on the path, now with the aerial mast on your right. Ignore a narrow path on your left and right. Just as the path descends, take a path on your right, which ascends. Cross another grass track and continue, close to the boundary fence to the mast on your right.

You will reach a sealed road. Cross the road and then take the path ahead and to your left. You will see the kiosk ahead in the distance. Head back to the kiosk, pass through the gate and descend to the car park.

6. Noar Hill

Medium - 2.5 miles - 2hr

This is a beautiful walk, which passes through a disused quarry, and is now a nature reserve. You will see many colourful wild flowers in the summer months, which attract lots of butterflies and bees. There are views as you ascend on the gentle path. The walk enters mixed deciduous woodland and then you will descend through another part of the nature reserve.

How to get there – From Petersfield, take the A3 and follow the sign for Guildford and London. Turn off the A3 when you see the sign for Selborne, on the B3006. Continue on this road into Selborne. Turn left, just after reaching the village, following the sign for Newton and Valence. Take the next road on the left, which is signed for Noar Hill. Shortly after passing the farm house on your left you will see the wide grass verge on your right, just before reaching Charity Farm Cottage on your right.

Grid Reference – SU 738322
Postcode – GU34 3LW

Parking – Free on the grass verge, just before reaching Charity Farm Cottage

Facilities – There are no facilities

You will need – Dog lead, dog bags and water for your dog

The Walk

❶ From the verge continue toward Charity Farm Cottage. Just before reaching the cottage take the bridleway on your left. This track is on part of the Hanger's Way long distance route. This is also an access track; therefore if you let your dog off the lead, listen out for traffic and horse riders.

Continue between the hedgerows, and after passing the field entrance you will begin to ascend. After a short ascent take a kissing gate on your right. ❷ This kissing gate is quite narrow, so for larger breeds of dog, you can continue a little further on the track and access the second kissing gate.

Keep your dog on the paths and under close control, as this is a wildlife reserve. There may be cattle grazing and ground-nesting birds in the nesting season. The site is a disused limestone quarry, which has been reclaimed by nature. Ascend now on the narrow path, through the grassland, with an abundance of wild flowers in the summer months.

There are many narrow paths, which make the route a little confusing. The important thing is to continue straight ahead, in the direction you were going, before entering into the reserve. Follow the most worn path as you continue to ascend, ignoring a minor path on your right. On seeing a kissing gate on your

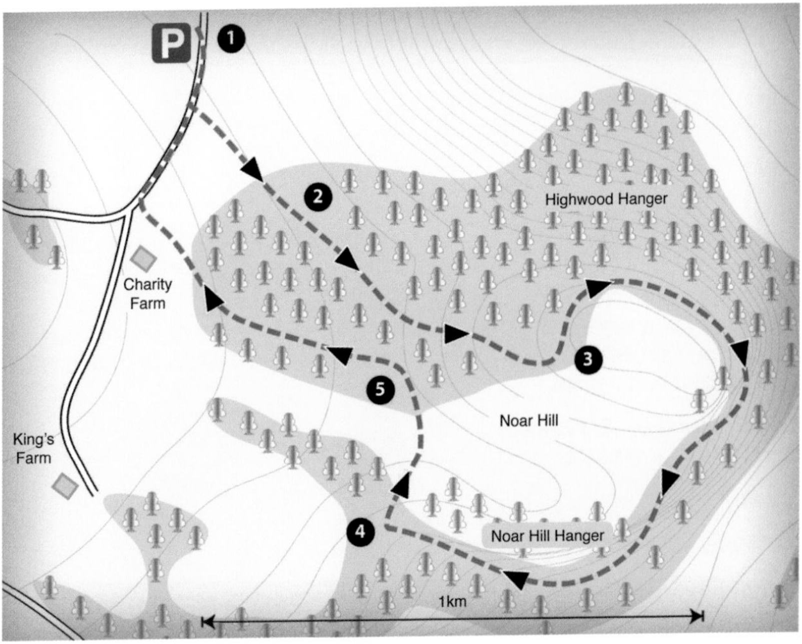

P
1
2
Highwood Hanger
Charity Farm
3
5
Noar Hill
King's Farm
4
Noar Hill Hanger
1km

far left turn right (this is the kissing gate for larger breeds of dog).

Ascend over a short steep hill. You will reach a fork just after, take the path on your left here. You will see an area ahead of you, looking into a small old quarry dug out with three sloping sides (now covered in grasses and flowers). There are views on your left. Walk along the top of the sloping side on your left, and continue to the far end of the reclaimed quarry workings.

You will reach an interpretation panel. Face the interpretation panel and turn left to continue on a worn grass path, which is undulating. ❸ You will soon be between trees. Continue on the path, and pass through some open glades, with many wild flowers. You will reach a stock fence on your right. Continue beside the fence for a short distance.

On reaching another path you will have views ahead, turn left here. Shortly after go through a gate and turn left. Continue through the woodland. When you reach another path and a fingerpost, turn right. Continue through the mixed broadleaved woods. The path is undulating, and a little further on it bends to your right. Continue on the wooded slope for quite a distance. On reaching another path turn right (the turn isn't obvious, and is more like merging to join another path straight ahead).

You now ascend through the woods. Continue passed a path on your right, and almost immediately pass a path on your left. Again almost immediately take the next path on your right, ❹ marked with a fingerpost signed bridleway. Descend, and as you continue you will be between banks, with a field beyond the trees on both sides.

Cross a track and continue straight ahead. You will be ascending now. On reaching a gate pass through it, to enter back into the Wildlife Trust Reserve. Ascend between the bramble, and on reaching another path turn left. ❺ Continue amongst the trees. You will reach a stock fence on your right, continue beside the fence.

After passing the stock fence the area opens up on your right, with beautiful wild flowers once again. Stay on the path, where you will have views ahead of the sloping fields. As you see a large rooftop ahead, you will descend. Ignore a minor path on your right.

You will reach a gate. Pass through the gate and descend between the trees. Keep your dog under close control, as you will reach a track. Turn right on the track. Put your dog on a lead, as you will soon reach a quiet road. Turn right on the road and continue, where you will pass Charity Farm Cottage, and then reach back to your car.

7. Selborne Common Chall - 3.6 miles 2hr 30min

This is a super circular walk, ascending to begin with on the zig zag path, which has lots of switch backs to lessen the gradient. Just two men dug out the path by hand in 1753. As you ascend the views are outstanding, extending across the countryside and hills. You will pass through beautiful heathland, with mixed woodland and standard trees. After passing through arable fields, and then a horse paddock, you will reach the church grounds and Newton Valence village. There is a beautiful village pond opposite to the church. A quiet track brings you back to the heathland and woods. There may be cattle grazing (of a gentle breed) and there is a stile (with a lift gate for dogs).

How to get there – From Petersfield, take the A3 and follow the sign for Guildford and London. Turn off the A3 when you see the sign for Selborne, on the B3006. Continue on this road into Selborne. The car park will be found on your left, and is sign posted.

Grid Reference – SU 741335
Postcode – GU34 3JR

Parking - Free

Facilities – There are toilets in the car park

You will need – Dog lead, dog bags

The Walk

❶ From the car park, take the path between the interpretation panel and the toilet block. Continue on this path, ascending gently between the hedgerows, with a horse paddock on your left. You will reach a kissing gate straight ahead. Go through the kissing gate, and enter into Selborne Common, and then turn left.

This is the start of your ascent, on the zig zags. The views will expand as you continue on the switchbacks. You will pass a bench as you near the top. Ignore the path on the right and continue on the steps. You will reach another bench at the top of the hill. Continue passed the bench and a small boulder on your right. Ascend the steps and pass beneath the trees.

You will join another wider path, with houses on your left. There may be cattle after passing through a kissing gate. The cattle are a gentle breed, which are used as a management tool, to graze the open areas, keeping them free of trees. On reaching the kissing gate, pass through it and continue straight ahead on the wide path. Pass through woodland, with open glades.

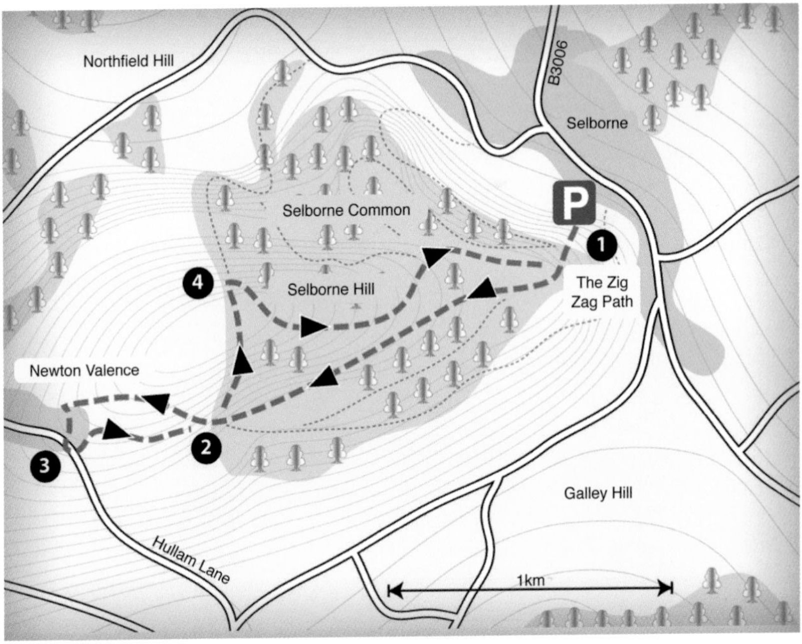

As you continue the area opens up, with a mix of gorse, bracken and trees.

When you reach near to the end of the open area, there is a fork. Take the path on your left. You will soon begin to descend gradually. When you reach a gate ahead, pass through it and take the narrow path on your right. ❷

Just after, go through the metal kissing gate and continue straight ahead, and cross through the field. Keep your dog under close control and stay on the path. On reaching the end of the field, pass through the gate beside the stile. Keep your dog under close control and continue straight ahead, across the horse paddock. You will reach a narrow end of the field. Ignore a gate on your left and cross the stile using the dog gate provided.

Continue between the garden fence and the trees. Pass beside a lovely old disused turnstile. Put your dog on a lead and enter into the church grounds. Pass between the yew trees. On reaching the gravel path, turn right. Go through the church gate and continue straight ahead to reach a road.

You will see the lovely village pond on the opposite side of the road. ❸ Turn left on the road, and take the bridleway on your left, just before reaching Pond Cottage. You will pass some houses on your left and there is a hedgerow on your right. After passing Manor House on your left it will be safe to let your dog off the lead, but beware of horse riders.

The path continues between trees, with fields on both sides beyond. At the end of the path you will reach a familiar spot. Pass through the gate, continue straight ahead and turn left just after. Continue on the woodland edge, with fields beyond the trees on your left.

On reaching a gate pass through it, and continue straight ahead. There may be cattle grazing. On reaching a fingerpost turn right, ❹ and follow the sign for permitted horse route (summer only for horses). Continue through the mixed broadleaved woodland. On reaching a gate pass through it and continue straight ahead. Shortly after the path appears to split, veer to your right. The path widens and you will pass a woodland pond on your left, just before you reach an opening.

Continue straight ahead, through the opening between the bracken. Stay on the wider path. Another wide path joins the path which you are on from your right. You are now on a familiar route. Continue straight ahead, passing through the woodland with glades. On reaching a kissing gate, pass through it and take the path on your left when you reach the fork. Take the path on your left, just before the boulder. Now descend the zig zags once again. Pass through the kissing gate on your right, and continue on the path to reach back to the car park.

8. Shortheath Common

Easy - 1.6 miles - 1hr

This is a lovely circular walk, on sandy paths through the common, which has a variety of habitats, including heathland, grassland and beautiful woodlands. There is also a fishing lake, where your dog can take a sneaky dip to cool off in an area away from the fishermen. There are many wild flowers in the summer months, which attract lots of butterflies.

How to get there – From Farnham, take the A31 towards Winchester. Turn off on the B3004, which is signed for Borden and Alton. Continue through Alton and East Worldham on the B3004 and turn right on reaching the sign for Oakhanger. The car park will be found on your left hand side before reaching Oakhanger. The postcode will take you to the Red Lion Pub in Oakhanger.

Grid Reference – SU 774369
Nearest Postcode – GU35 9JQ

Parking – Free

Facilities – There are no facilities

You will need – Dog leads, dog bags

The Walk

❶ From the car park, face the road and turn right. Stay in the car park, where you will reach a path. There is a fishing lake on your right. Take the right path on reaching the fork, following beside the edge of the lake. There is mixed woodland and gorse.

Continue straight ahead as you join another path from your left and behind. You will pass beside pockets of heathland on your left. A little further along, after passing the lake the area opens up, with some heathland on your right. The path veers to your left and joins another path.

Just after, on reaching another path turn right, and continue through the woods. On reaching a fork, take the path on your right. The path will widen and the heath opens out, with grasses, bracken and gorse. Continue on the main path, and cross the open area. You will reach back into the woods for a short distance.

You will reach a mown area of the common. Cross this and then enter back into the woods, where you will need to put your dog on a lead or under close control, as there is an access track and village green ahead. ❷ On reaching the track turn left, with the common now on your left.

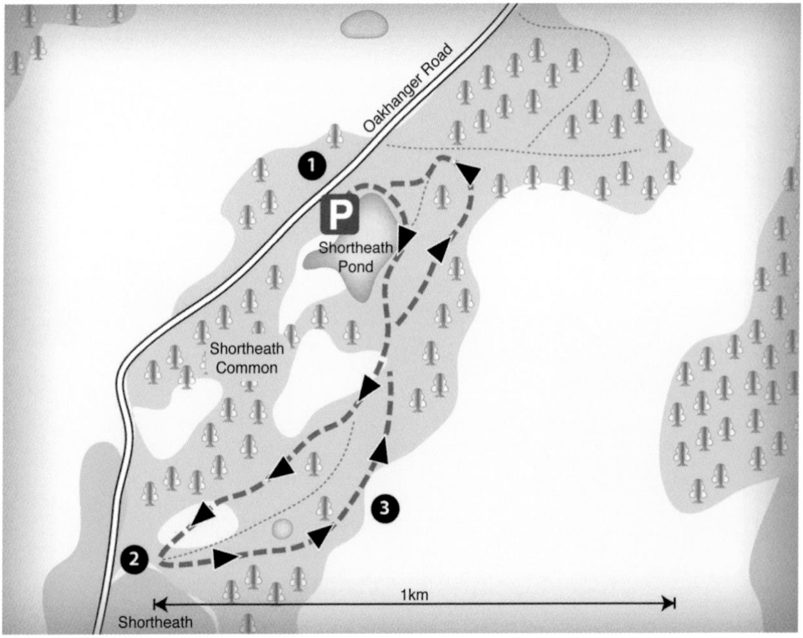

You will pass some houses and a builders yard on your right. You will then pass a driveway on your right, where you continue straight ahead, ascending with trees on both sides of the track. On reaching a fork turn left. Pass a track on your right and take a path on your left, just as you see a thatched cottage. Join another track shortly after, where you continue straight ahead.

On reaching another track turn right, where you will see an open grass field on your left. Continue on this access track between the trees. You will pass a wet area on your right. Soon after take a track on your left. You can now let your dog off the lead, as there is no access to vehicles. The trees become widely spaced here, with pockets of grassland. There are many butterflies in the summer months.

The path veers to your left and you will enter back into oak and silver birch woodland. ❸ Pass a gate and a house (currently dilapidated) on your right. Ignore a path on your left. The path will bend to your left, and you will pass a clearing on your left. Keep to your right, ignoring a path on your left.

On reaching another path turn right. You are now on a familiar path. Ignore a path on your left and continue straight ahead, where you will leave the familiar path behind (you can take the path on your left to retrace your steps back to the car park, if you want to shorten your walk). Ignore another path on your left.

A little further along, the trees become widely spaced. There is heather on your left and on your right there are grasses. Continue on the sandy path between the gorse. Pass a metal post. You will reach another track; turn left here with a garden fence on your right. You will pass Heathfield House on your right. Continue straight ahead. As the track bends to your left, ignore a track on your right and continue straight on.

As the track bends to your left again (also with a track on your right) take the narrow path on your left. Pass a pylon on your right. On reaching the fishing lake turn right and retrace your steps back to the car park.

9. Alice Holt Forest VC

Med - 2.6 miles - 2hrs

This forested circular walk is popular with families, as there are play areas and picnic sites. The forest tracks are well-made and offer some shade for your dog on hot days. There is a short, moderate ascent at the end of this walk. There are many butterflies in summer and wild flowers on the sides of the path. There are no roads or livestock, although there may be wild deer in the area.

How to get there – From Farnborough join the A331 and follow the signs for Farnham. Join the A31 and continue to follow the sign for Farnham. Continue on the A31 and follow the sign for Winchester and Alton on the Farnham by-pass. On reaching a roundabout, turn left on the A325, following the sign for Petersfield and Wrecclesham. Continue on this road, where you will pass Forest Lodge Garden Centre. Turn left when you see the brown sign for Alice Holt Forest. Continue on this road for a short distance and turn left on reaching the Forest sign.

Grid Reference – SU 810414 **Postcode** – GU10 4LS

Parking – Pay and Display Forestry Commission car park

Facilities – There are toilets and a café

You will need – Dog lead, dog bags

The Walk

❶ This walk starts at the toilet block, near to the visitor centre. From the toilet block stand with your back to the entrance to the toilets facing the building opposite. Turn left and head towards a car park. Cross the car park, passing the pay and display on your left. Take the path on the opposite side and follow the blue waymarkers. Silver birch trees dominate this section of the woods.

On reaching another path at the bend, turn right. Descend on the path through mixed broadleaved and conifer woods. On reaching another path, turn left and shortly after turn right. Descend the steps through the conifer forest.

Descend another set of steps and cross a small stream. ❷ Your dog can get water here. Ascend some steps and continue; now ascending gently. The forest changes from conifer with mixed broadleaved trees, to predominantly broadleaved woods. Bracken dominates the woodland floor.

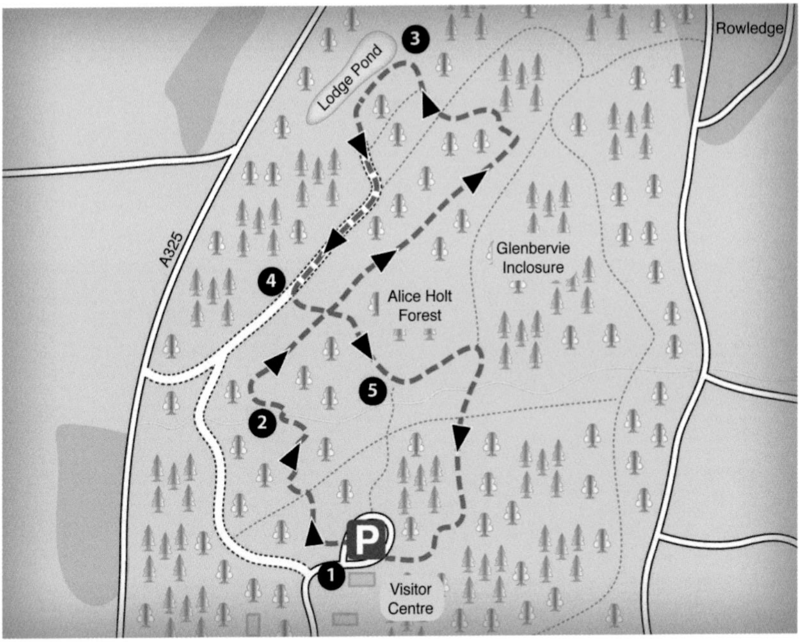

Cross another path and continue straight ahead. You will pass a woodland glade on your left. You will ascend gently on the path for a while. Turn left on a path, where you see the blue waymarker. Pass through a barrier and turn left. Cross another wide track and continue straight ahead, but veering slightly to

your left. This path is signed for Lodge Pond. You will soon see the pond straight ahead.

Cross a path to reach the pond. ❸ Your dog can cool off on a hot day, providing he can access the water without disturbing the fishermen. Turn left on the path beside the pond. Ignore a path on your left and continue beside the pond. Take the next path on your left, which is signed by the blue way-marker.

Keep your dog under close control. You will pass a picnic area on your left, and then you will reach a car park. Continue through the car park and follow on the track which bends to your left, and soon after the track bends to your right and merges with another track (don't turn left here). There is an open area on your left. Continue on the gravel track, which is an access road for the car park; keep your dog on a lead or under close control.

❹ Take the next turning on your left, which is a wide path rather than a track. You will have bracken and trees on both sides. Continue passed paths on your left and right, which are also marked by blue way-markers. Descend on the path and turn right soon after. Descend on this path, which is more enclosed and shaded. On reaching another path you will see a giant wooden owl on your right. ❺ Turn left on this path. You will pass various wooden sculptures along the way now.

On reaching another path turn right. Descend and then ascend immediately after. Ignore a path on your right, just after the wooden tubes on your right. You will soon ascend, gently at first, and then there is a short steep section. As you reach near to the top of the hill, ignore two right hand paths, which lead to a wooden play structure. Take the next right path immediately after, on reaching the top of the hill. You will pass the play structure on your right, beyond the trees. Ignore a left and right turn immediately after passing the play structure. Continue on the path where you will pass a car park on your right and shortly after you will see the toilet block on your left.

10. Alice Holt Forest North   Easy - 2 miles - 1hr 30min

This circular walk is perfect if you are looking for shade for your dog, on those hot summer days as it is within the forest. The forest tracks are well-made and there are many butterflies in the summer months, which fly amongst the wild flowers on each side of the path. Your dog can enjoy time off the lead, as there are no livestock, however wild deer may be in the area. There are no roads, but the forest tracks may from time to time have forest machinery in operation.

How to get there –From Farnborough join the A331 and follow the signs for Farnham. Join the A31 and continue to follow the sign for Farnham. Continue on the A31 and follow the sign for Winchester and Alton on the Farnham by-pass. On reaching a roundabout, turn left on the A325 following the sign for Petersfield and Wrecclesham. Continue on this road, where you will pass Forest Lodge Garden Centre. Take the next turning on your right shortly after, which is signposted for the Forestry Commission Research Centre. You will pass the Alice Holt Research Centre on your left. Continue straight ahead, where you will pass a JCB plant on your right. Take the next turn on your left, which is marked by a fingerpost, where you will reach the car park.

Grid Reference – SU 802434 **Nearest Postcode** – GU10 4LG

Parking –Free in Forestry Commission car park

Facilities – There are no facilities

You will need – Dog leads, dog bags and water for your dog

The Walk

❶ From the car park, pass beside the vehicle barrier and continue into the mixed broadleaved woods. Continue on the gravel track, and ignore paths on your left and right. After a while you will reach a tarmac path. Cross this path and continue on the track straight ahead. There is an area on your right which has been clear felled and left to naturally regenerate.

Ignore paths on your left and right and continue straight ahead. The trees here are mostly conifer, with thick laurel understory. There is a fence line on your left, which is a tree inclosure to keep deer out. You will descend on the path. Just as you reach the end of the tree inclosure on your left you will pass a path on your right. ❷

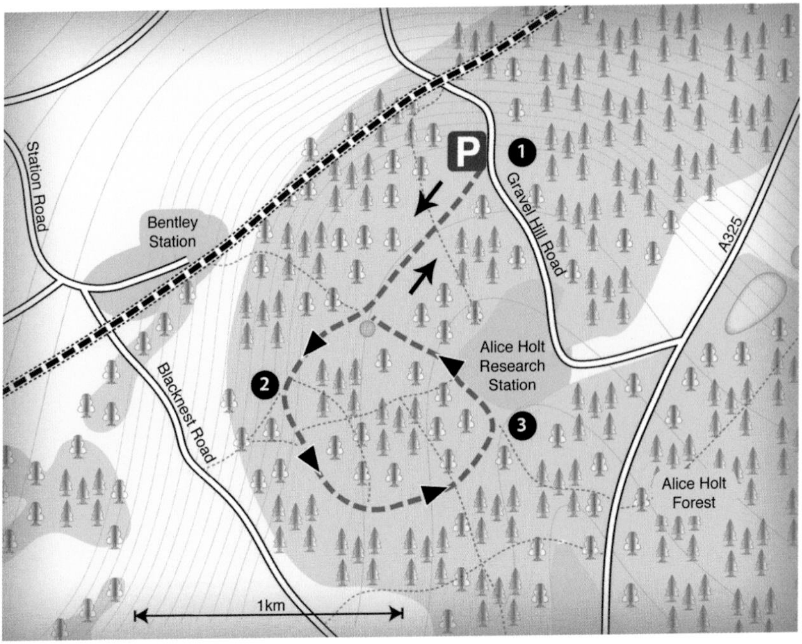

You will ascend on the path for a short distance. You will pass a forest clearing on your left, which has also been left to naturally regenerate. A little further along the woodland is dominated by conifer trees. Soon after another ascent, ignore a path on your right and continue straight ahead. There is another inclosure on your left, with natural regenerated trees within it. On reaching another path turn left. ❸ You are now on a section of the Shipwrights Way, which is a long distance route.

There is an inclosure on your right and silver birch trees are regenerating on your left. After passing the inclosure, ignore a grass path on your left. There is an enclosed meadow just beyond the trees. Beyond the meadow you will see the Alice Holt Lodge Research Station, keep your dog under close control or on a lead here. Soon after, pass beside a vehicle barrier where you will reach a quiet road. There is a row of houses ahead.

Turn left on the road where you will pass a small meadow on your right. You will then continue into the woods on the tarmac road. After a while you will pass an enclosed pond on your left. Just after passing the pond on your left, take the path on your right. You are now on a familiar path which will eventually reach back to the car park.

11. Old Winchester Hill Medium - 2.5 miles - 2hr

This is a wonderful circular walk having fabulous views right from the start. The hill fort, known as Old Winchester Hill can be clearly seen as it stands out in the landscape. You will walk beside wonderful floristic meadows, with many butterflies throughout the walk. On reaching the hill fort, a path will guide you around the perimeter on the outer ramparts, where you will have excellent panoramic views. You will pass through woodland, and then ascend on a steep slope to finish your walk. There may be ground nesting birds such as skylarks, and sheep grazing, therefore keep your dog on a lead or under very close control and stay on the footpaths.

How to get there – From Petersfield, take the A272, following the sign for Winchester. Veer left when reaching the sign for the A32, sign posted to Farnham. On reaching West Meon, take the second road on your left, which is Station Road. At the end of this road turn left. Continue on this road, where you will reach the car park on the right hand side of the road.

Grid Reference – SU 645214

Parking – Free in car park

Facilities – There are no facilities

You will need – Dog lead, dog bags and water for your dog

The Walk

❶ From the entrance of the car park, ignore the first gate on your left, and as the car park widens take the next gate on your left. There is an interpretation panel inside a hut ahead and to your right. Don't take the path ahead, but take the path on your left before reaching the hut, passing another interpretation panel on your right. Continue on the stone path between the scrub.

Soon after on reaching an opening you will have wonderful views across the sloped grassland to the ancient hill fort on your right. During the end of March and until the end of July please keep your dog on the paths, as there may be ground-nesting birds here. After a few yards, ignore the wide grass path straight ahead and turn right. Descend a short distance, where you will reach another grass path. Turn left on this path and continue through the meadow. The road is on your far left; so ensure that your dog doesn't stray to the road.

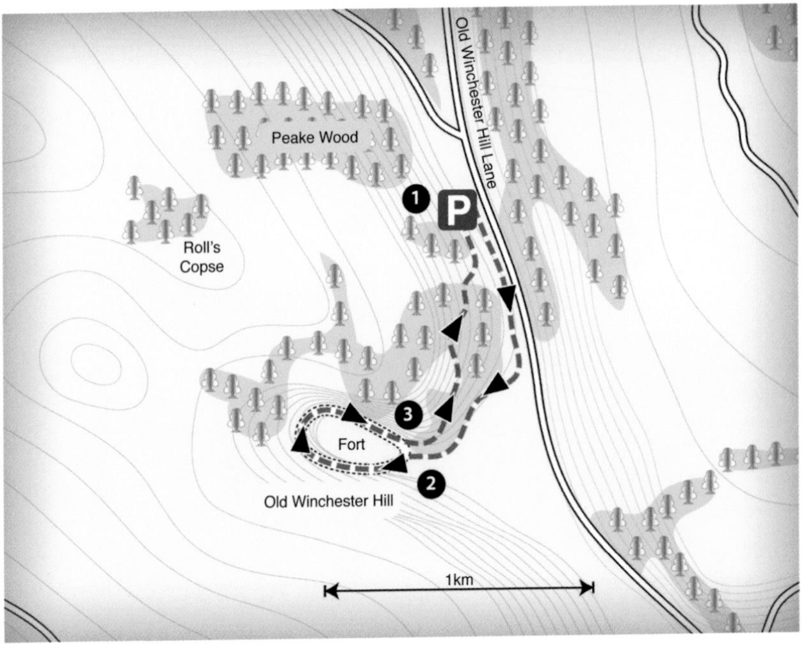

A little further on, the wide path, and the path which you are on will merge briefly. Continue on the lower path on your right. The path will soon veer to your right and away from the road. There is scrub now on your right, which obscure the views. You will reach a stone track, where

you turn right, now on part of the South Downs Way (SDW) long distance footpath. Continue on the path, which is signed for the hill fort, beside the stock fence on your left. There is a field on your left and trees on your right. Ignore a couple of paths on your right. You will pass a couple of benches where you can enjoy the views, and soon you will descend gently.

Ignore a footpath on your left, where you now leave the SDW. Pass through a gate straight ahead, and continue passed an interpretation panel and a bench. ❷ Veer to your left, where you will follow around the base of the hill fort. Ignore a path on your right and continue, now on the rampart of the hill fort. You will have endless, stunning views in all directions, across wonderful farmland and woodlands. Beautiful flowers grow on the sides of the rampart, adding colour in the summer months, and attracting many butterflies and bees. You may also hear the sound of the yellow hammer singing in summer.

As you continue, ignore a path on your left and right, and continue on the rampart, on the well-worn path. When you reach back to the bench and gate, don't go through the gate, but turn left, ❸ descending with some steps along the way (if you want a shorter walk, continue through the gate and retrace your steps).

Continue on the chalk white path which is undulating, with trees on your right and a flower rich grass bank on your left (depending on the time of year). There are stunning views on your left. On meeting another path turn left, and continue to descend. The path becomes quite steep. Pass through a kissing gate and enter into woodland. Stay on the worn path, which snakes through the mixed broadleaved woods. Descend on the path, with some steps in places.

On reaching the edge of the woods pass through the kissing gate, ensuring that your dog is under close control as there may be livestock and ground nesting birds. Continue through the floristic meadows, following the chalk path. The path will ascend and when the chalk path ends turn right, ascending the steep bank on a grass path.

On reaching the top of the hill, pass through a kissing gate and turn right. Ignore the path on your right almost immediately and continue straight ahead. You will reach the hut, with the interpretation panels inside on your left. Continue straight ahead, where you will reach back to the car park.

12. West Meon

Medium - 5.12 miles - 3hrs

On this circular walk you will pass over part of an old disused railway. There are woodlands on both sides for much of the way. The second half of the walk is on part of the South Downs Way long distance route, and you will pass through farmland, with fencing on both sides to keep your dog away from livestock. There is also some arable farmland. Stunning views can be seen on a clear day across the rolling hills. The paths are undulating, with some gradual ascents.

How to get there – From Winchester, take the A31, which is signed for Petersfield (A272). Continue on the A272, until reaching the traffic lights. Turn right at the lights onto the A32, and continue into West Meon. On reaching West Meon, take the second road on your left, which is Station Road. The car park will be located on the right hand side of the road, just before going over the railway bridge.

Grid Reference – SU 641236 **Nearest Postcode** – GU32 1JJ

Parking – Free in the car park

Facilities – There are no facilities

You will need – Dog lead, dog bags and water for your dog

The Walk

❶ Continue to the furthest end of the car park and pass the interpretation panel. Continue on the path of the old disused railway, with banks on both sides. There may be horse riders and cyclists on this path. As you continue, the path will become more exposed, as you pass the banks on both sides. There are trees, which line the path, with fields beyond on both sides.

Ignore a path on your right, and continue on the railway. There are banks on both sides once again. You will pass under a road bridge. You will now be on a bank, looking down through the trees to the fields below. Keep your dog under close control, as there is a quiet road ahead, without a boundary fence. Ensure you have your dog on a lead before you descend on the path to reach the road. Cross the road and continue on the railway straight ahead.

❷ On reaching a fingerpost turn left and follow the sign for the South Downs Way (SDW) long distance footpath. The footpath has a switch back. Look behind for views. There is a hedge on your right and a stock fence on your left, with a field beyond it.

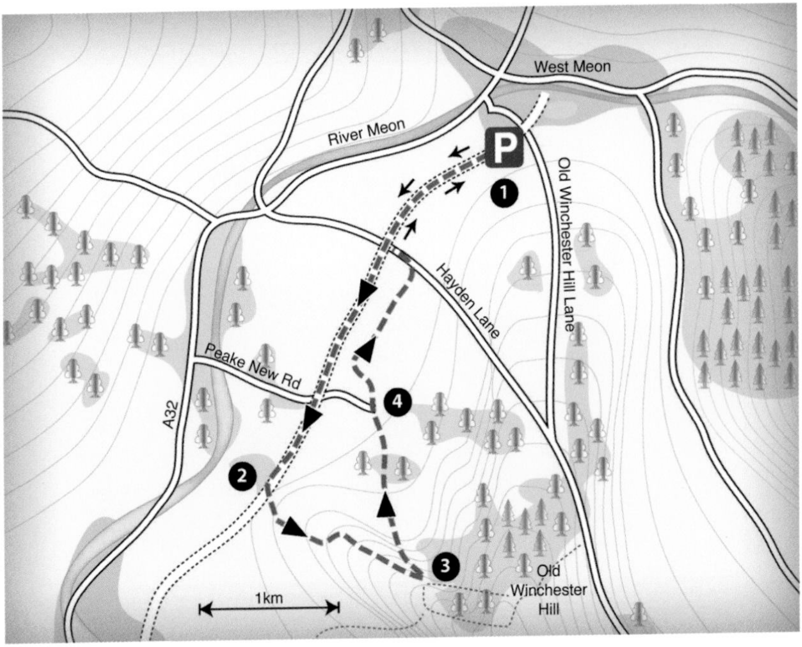

The path soon ascends gradually, and then it will become a little steeper as you continue. Follow several bends, as you continue passing around corners in the fence line on your left. There are views on your right in places where there are breaks in the hedge.

❸ On reaching a fingerpost turn left, where you join the Monarch's Way and leave the SDW. The path descends on the edge of a field, which is fenced and there is a hedgerow on your right. A break in the hedge allows views on your right. As you turn a bend you will be on the edge of a field on your right. Keep your dog under close control avoiding possible damage to the crops. There is a wildflower strip before the crops, where there may be ground-nesting birds. There are wonderful views on your right and a hedge on your left.

At the end of the field you will join another track, continue straight ahead. Put your dog on a lead, or under close control on this access track. Ignore a path immediately right and pass a pond on your right. Continue on the track, which is concrete to begin with. Ignore a track on your left soon after. Continue between the stock fences, with fields on each side. The field on your right is woodland pasture at first.

On reaching a sharp bend on the path and a fingerpost, turn left and then immediately right. Follow on the edge of a field, with a hedgerow on your right. Shortly after you will pass beside farm buildings on your right. Go through a gap in the hedge, passing the fingerpost.

❹ Turn left on the quiet access track. After passing an access road on your right, take the footpath on your right. Continue between the horse fields. Cross a path at the end of the fence line on your left and continue straight ahead. Cross a footbridge over a ditch and then turn left. Now follow the quiet lane between horse paddocks. Keep your dog on a lead, or under close control as there may be traffic accessing the equestrian centre.

Continue on the track for quite some distance. On reaching a road put your dog on a lead and turn left. Descend on the road, and cross the bridge over the disused railway. Take the footpath on your right immediately after, where you will descend beside the old railway below on your right. On reaching the railway turn left and retrace your steps back to the car park.

13. West Walk

Easy - 1.9 miles - 1hr 30min

This short circular walk is within the forest on well-made paths, and follows a well-marked route. There are plantations of coniferous trees and also some mixed broadleaved trees. There are no livestock but there may be deer in the area. The paths are undulating, but for the last section there is a moderate ascent. This walk is fun for children too, as there are woodland play areas. There are no livestock and no roads.

How to get there – From the M27 take the turn off at junction 10, signed for the A32 and Alton. At the Wickham roundabout, continue straight ahead on the A32. Turn right onto the B2177, signed for Southwick. Turn left at the sign for Hundred Acres and New Town on Hundred Acre road. The car park will be located on your left hand side, signed Forestry Commission, West Walk.

Grid Reference – SU 597122

Nearest Postcode – PO17 6JD

Parking – Pay and Display

Facilities – There are toilets in the car park

You will need – Dog leads, dog bags

The Walk

❶ Keep your dog on a lead to begin with. Start this walk from the interpretation panel, with the toilet block on your right. Continue straight ahead, on the well-made path. On meeting another track turn left and follow the sign for West Walk. Pass an enclosed play area on your left and an open play area on your right.

Descend gently and ignore a narrow path on your right, and then pass a picnic area. Continue on the wide gravel path, which soon descends a little steeper. On reaching a bend keep left, following the sign for West Walk, ignoring the track on your right. Ignore a path on your left immediately after and continue. The path descends gradually. Ignore a narrow path on your right.

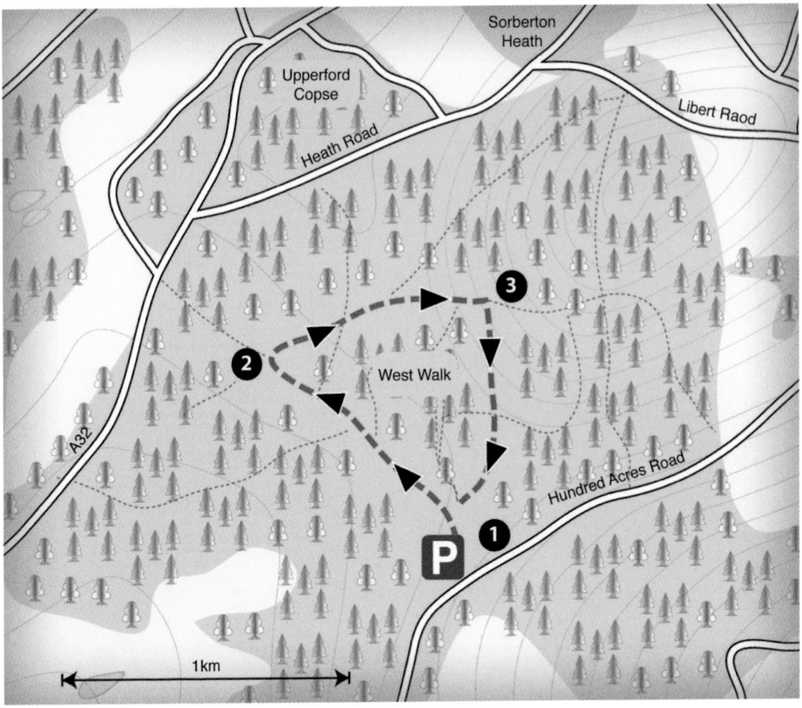

Continue through the mixed broadleaved woodland, with bracken on each side of the path. Ignore a narrow path on your right a little further along. On meeting another path, ❷ turn right and continue to follow the sign for West Walk. Ignore any minor paths on your left and right and continue on the wide track. Ignore a

path on your left, signed for Woodend and descend on the wide track.

The track ascends slightly and there is a right hand bend. Ignore a path on your left at the bend. The path levels off again. Take the next track on your right, ❸ which is signed for West Walk. There is a water hole for your dog on the left and right of the path shortly after. The path then ascends gently.

Take a path on your left, which ascends a little steeply, signed West Walk. As you ascend a little further the open play area is on your right. You will soon reach back to the car park.

14. Droxford

Easy - 2.2 miles - 1hr 30min

This is a wonderful circular walk, which crosses the lovely River Meon, where your dog can have a drink and a dip. Continue across lovely farmland meadows and between arable fields, where there are floristic strips to encourage wildlife. After crossing a quiet country lane you will reach a disused railway. In the summer months you will hear skylarks, and see many bees and butterflies. There is a short stretch of quiet country road and there may be livestock for a short section of the walk.

How to get there – From the M27 between Southampton and Portsmouth take the turn-off at junction 10, which is sign-posted for the A32 Alton. Continue on this road, following the sign for Alton. Before reaching Alton you will reach Droxford. Once in the village you will see the village hall car park on your right.

Grid Reference – SU 606182
Postcode – SO32 3RB

Parking – Free in the village hall car park

Facilities – There are no facilities

You will need – Dog lead, dog bags

The Walk

❶ Keep your dog on a lead to begin this walk. From the car park go to the furthest end from the road and enter into the church grounds. Leave the gravel path where it bends to your right. Continue on a grass path passing a fingerpost, signed Wayfarer's Walk and Emsworth. On reaching a kissing gate, don't go through it, but turn right. Follow the slab path. On leaving the church grounds, turn left on the path between trees. You can let your dog off the lead here.

Pass through a kissing gate on reaching it. Keep your dog under close control, as there may be livestock. Your dog can get access to the river here to the left of the footbridge, providing it is not to fast flowing. Cross the footbridge over the River Meon and continue straight ahead, between fields. In the summer months there is meadow sweet on your right. Cross another footbridge and continue straight ahead, ignoring the footpath on your right.

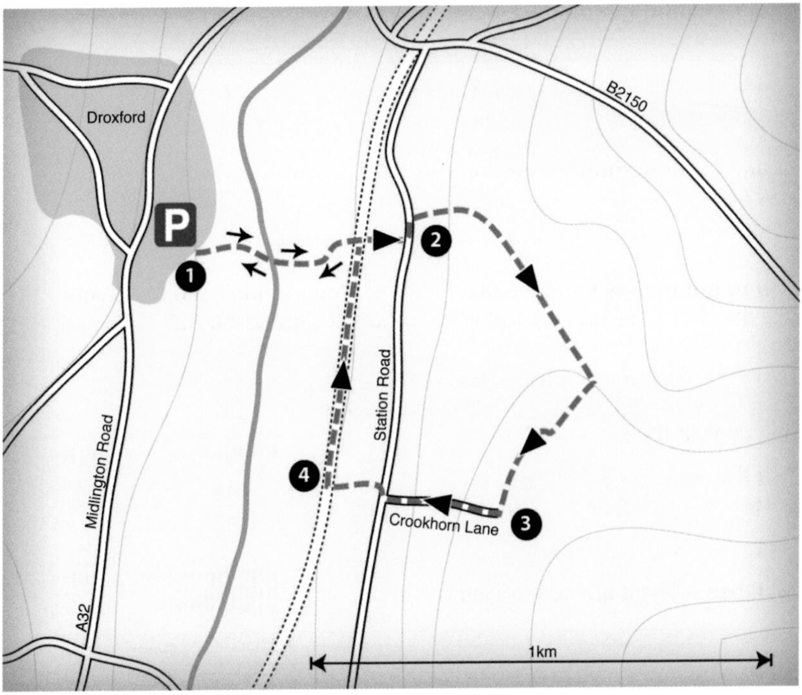

Continue on the edge of the field beside nettles on your right. On reaching the end of the field, pass through the kissing gate. Continue straight ahead, ignoring the path on your left. Ascend a short distance and then pass through another kissing gate. Turn left on the field edge. At the end of the field pass through another kissing gate. Put your dog on a lead and ascend between the barbed wire fences on an access track.

Cross a railway bridge and continue between the garden fences where you will reach a quiet road. Turn left on the road. After passing the driveway for Greylands, turn right on the footpath. ❷ Cross a stile, which has one step, and platform, making it easy for your dog, there is also a gap where your dog can squeeze through. Keep your dog on the path under close control, as there may be ground-nesting birds. Continue straight ahead, on the edge of the field, beside the hedgerow on your right.

As you reach the end of the hedgerow on your right you will have beautiful views. The path bends to your right, with flower strips on both sides in the summer months. Continue through the middle of a large arable field. On reaching a track turn right. ❸ Continue between the fields and follow the track as it bends sharply to the right and then left.

You are now between hedgerows. Ignore a stile at the next bend, and continue on the track. Put your dog on a lead here, as you will pass several driveways to houses. On reaching a road turn right. Look out for a footpath on your left shortly after. Pass through the kissing gate and continue between the hedge and fence. On reaching an old railway bridge don't go under it, but turn right and ascend to the disused railway, and turn right. ❹

Continue between hedges and trees, and beware of horse riders and cyclists on the path. Take a path on your left just as you reach an arched bridge. Ascend with some steps. You will reach a familiar track, turn left here and retrace your steps. Pass through the kissing gate, staying on the edge of the field, again keep your dog under close control. Pass through another two kissing gates and continue on the edge of the field. Cross the footbridges once again, where your dog can cool off, before reaching the church grounds and then back to your car.

15. Beacon Hill

Easy - 1.7 miles - 1hrs

This is a short linear walk to Beacon Hill, which is an Iron Age hill fort. There are stunning views across the beautiful countryside, with patchwork fields and woodlands. In the summer months the chalk grassland is abundant with colourful flowers, where bees and butterflies are plentiful. During the nesting season (end of February – end July) there may be rare ground nesting birds, so it is best to keep your dog on the paths whilst amongst the grassland. There may be cattle at certain times of the year, but there are no roads.

How to get there - From Winchester follow the sign for Petersfield (A272) on the B3404. Continue on the A272 signed for Petersfield and turn right when you see the sign for Warnford and Preshaw. At the junction continue straight ahead, following the sign for West Meon and Preshaw. Continue straight ahead crossing another road junction following signs for Preshaw, Warnford and West Meon. You will pass the turn off for Preshaw, and continue straight ahead. As you pass some agricultural buildings on your left, turn right at the crossroads. Continue on this road, where you will find the car park amongst the trees on your left at the bend in the road.

Grid Reference – SU 598227

Parking – Free

You will need – Dog leads, dog bags and water for your dog

The Walk

❶ From the car park, face the road and turn left. Go through the gate and pass the interpretation panel. Continue on the path, which is part of the South Downs Way (SDW) long distance route. The path is lined with beech trees on your left. There is a stock fence on your right, with a field beyond. As you continue there is mixed broadleaved woodland on your left. There are views on your right to the sea and the Isle of White.

Pass a trig point on your right. ❷ On reaching a fingerpost continue straight ahead, where you leave the SDW. There are views on your right. Continue to a farm gate and go through the kissing gate. Descend on the path between the nettles, with woods on your left. You will have wonderful views here. As you continue there are wild flowers in the summer months on your right.

The woods are set back now on your left and there are wild flowers on both sides. During the nesting season it is best to keep your dog on the path to protect ground-nesting birds. Ignore a path on your right and continue straight ahead. The path bends to your left and descends. You will reach another path where you have wonderful views across the countryside. Turn right and descend.

You will see the ancient hill fort ramparts clearly here. Take a path on your left which descends quite steeply. Continue on the path, around the outer rampart. The path will peter out. ❸ Simply turn around and retrace your steps.

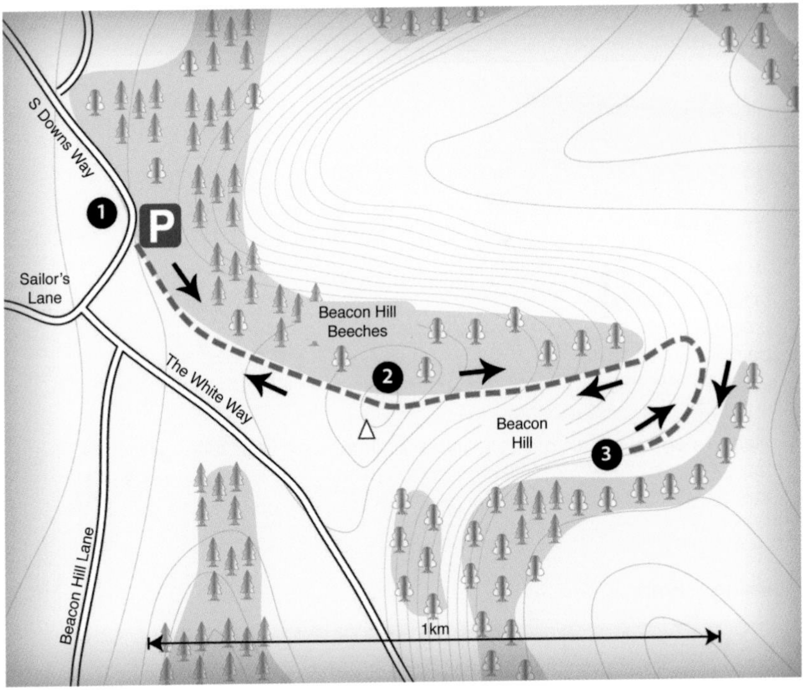

16. Longwood Warren

Medium - 3.6 miles - 2hr

This walk is very picturesque, with many wild flowers in the summer months. The views are outstanding across the surrounding area, with miles of beautiful countryside. The flint and chalk paths are well made and undulating, as you cross the arable farmland. You will pass on the edge of a meadow and then enter into mixed broadleaved and coniferous woodland.

How to get there – From Winchester take the A31 and follow the sign for Petersfield (A272). Continue to follow the Petersfield signs, where you will join the A272. Continue on the A272 for about a mile, where you will see the car park on your right.

Grid Reference – SU 528277

Parking – Free in the car park

Facilities – There are no facilities

You will need – Dog lead, dog bags and water for your dog

The Walk

❶ Put your dog on a lead to begin this walk. From the car park go back to the busy road and turn right on the grass verge. On reaching a gate on your right and a fingerpost cross the road and pass through the gap beside the gate. Continue on the path, which is part of the South Downs Way (SDW) long distance path. You will be between arable fields.

After crossing the field turn left on the worn path just before the fingerpost. ❷ You now leave the SDW. There are hawthorn trees and fields. You will have wonderful views on your right after passing the trees. You will descend on the path and pass through a gap in the fence to enter into a field. Continue on the edge of the field with a hedgerow on your left.

There are wild flower strips on your right, just before the arable field. On reaching a track turn left and ascend. On reaching another track turn right. There are amazing views on your right of sloping countryside. There is a good colourful mix of wild flowers on each side of the path in the summer months.

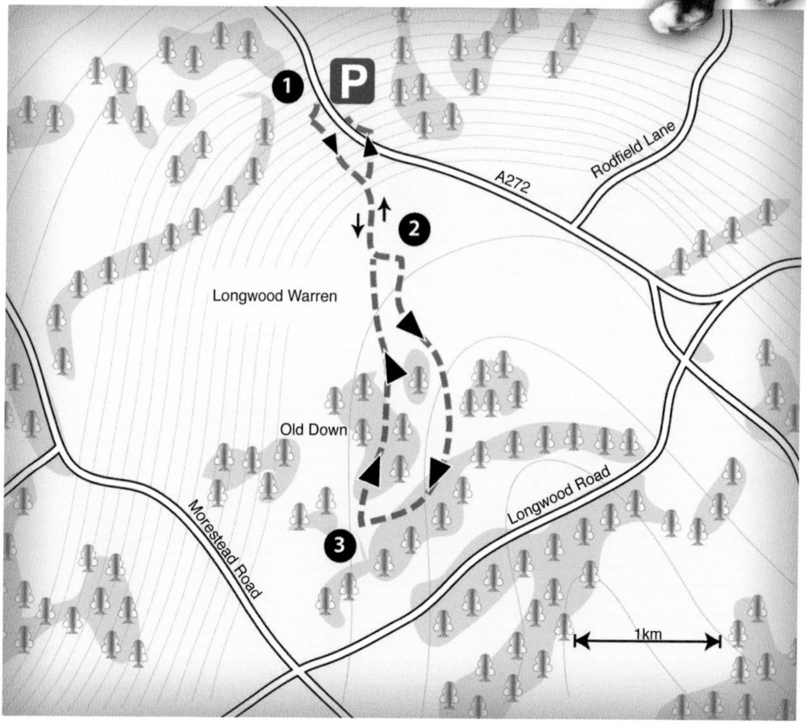

Descend on the path for some distance, keeping your dog on the path. There are views ahead and on your left as you continue. On reaching a way-marker and a track on your left, take this track, descending between arable fields. On reaching the end of the field on your right, turn right onto a narrow path. You will now be on the edge of a field, with a stock fence and a hedgerow on your left.

At the end of the fence line on your left continue straight ahead, passing double gates on your right. There is a large field of crops ahead and left. You are now walking on the edge of a field, which is on your left and a stock fence on your right with a field beyond it. Just before reaching a green shipping container take a footpath on your right. Keep your dog on a lead or under close control, as there may be livestock. Pass through the gate and continue on the path at the edge of a field, there is a woodland block on your left.

On reaching the end of the woodland block on your left, there is a fence line and an arable field. On reaching a gate pass through it and cross a track, continue straight ahead, where you will enter into hazel and hawthorn dominated woodland. Continue passed a field entrance, where the path becomes a track.

On reaching a wider track turn right. Continue through the woods. When you reach the end of the track turn right, ❸ and ascend gradually. There is a hedgerow on your left with a floristic verge and a small field on your right. At the end of the fields you will continue on a track between the woods.

On reaching a fingerpost turn right, on the woodland track through the coppice woodland. Ignore a path on your right soon after. Ascend gradually on the path. On reaching a gate pass through it and continue straight ahead on the field edge, with woods on your left. There is a wild flower strip on your right. Ascend gently on the path.

On reaching a wider track continue straight ahead. Ascend on this track for some distance, between arable fields, with floristic strips on both sides. Ignore a footpath on your right. You are now back on a familiar path. Continue on the gentle ascent, and put your dog on a lead, as there is a road ahead. Ignore the footpath on your left and continue to the small gate ahead. Cross the road and turn left on the grass verge, where you will soon reach your car.

17. Avington

Medium - 2.5 miles - 2hrs

This circular walk is very picturesque, and starts with a view across the lake to Avington Lodge, which was built in the late 16th Century. You will walk through meadows and along glorious clear waters of the River Itchen, where your dog can cool off on hot days. You will cross a couple of road bridges on the quiet lanes, and then pass through Avington Village. There may be livestock on parts of this walk and there are some quiet country lanes. There is plenty of water for your dog along the way.

How to get there - From Winchester take the A31, signed for Petersfield and Alresford. Turn left when you see the sign for Avington and Itchen Abbas. On reaching Avington turn left, following the sign for Easton and Winchester. You will see the car park on your right at little further along the road.

Grid Reference – SU 528320

Parking – Free in the car park

Facilities – There are no facilities

You will need – Dog lead, dog bags

The Walk

❶ From the car park, face away from the road and go to the left hand side of the car park. Take the narrow path which heads away from the road. Pass between the mature trees and continue on the grass path on the edge of a meadow, with trees on your right.

Pass beside an old kissing gate where you will see a lake with Avington Lodge beyond it. Turn left and follow the worn grass path, beside the stock fence on your left. Go through a kissing gate on your left, and continue on the grass path at the edge of a meadow, with a fence on your right. Keep your dog under close control, as there may be livestock and there is a road ahead. If the grass is long, the road will be obscured as it passes through the middle of the meadow, and not on the boundary as it may appear.

On reaching the quiet road turn right. Pass through a gate to avoid the cattle grid and continue on the road. There are woods on both sides of the road. As the road descends, pass a beautifully designed house on your right. Pass a house on your left, and just after take the footpath on your right which crosses a bridge over a river. ❷

Continue on the gravel path between the trees. There is a barbed wire fence and wetlands on your right, and a stock fence on your left. Cross another footbridge over beautiful clear water. There are now wetland plants on both

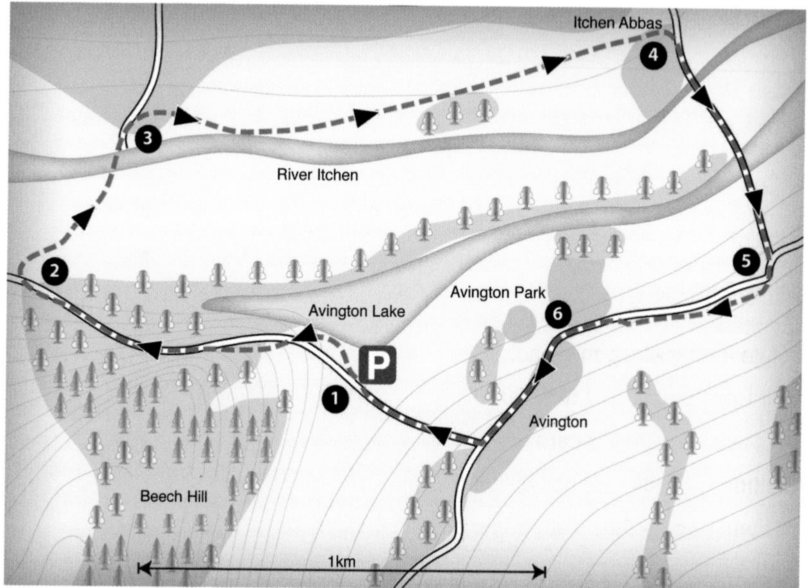

sides of the path. You will reach a wide area of the River Itchen. Check the flow of the river before you allow your dog to take a dip.

Put your dog on a lead before you cross the footbridge over the river, which is a beautiful sight, with clear water and plant life. Follow on the path, beside the garden on your right. Pass between houses and ignore the narrow road/lane on your left. Take the footpath on your right just after, which is indicated by a fingerpost. ❸

Ascend the steps and continue on the gravel path beside a red brick wall and a garden fence. As you reach the end of the garden on your left, ignore the footpath on your left. Continue straight ahead passing a pony paddock. Go through a kissing gate and ignore the footpath on your left. You now follow beside the beautiful River Itchen on your right. It is worth stopping for a while and letting your dog enjoy the water, providing the flow is not too strong.

Continue on the path beside the narrow meadow. There are also meadows on your left, beyond the post and rail fence and some houses on your far left. The path veers away from the river. Pass through a gate straight ahead, keeping your dog on a lead, as there may be pigs here. Continue beside the fence line on your left, where after crossing the field, you will pass through another gate.

Cross a track, and go through the kissing gate ahead. Follow on the path between brambles with a field on your right. You will pass houses and gardens on your left. Pass through a gate and turn left onto a track, putting your dog on a lead. Pass beside houses on your right on a gravel driveway. On reaching a road turn right. ❹

Go passed a flint stone church on your right and a house on your left. Cross a couple of bridges over canalised sections of diverted river, and then cross another bridge over the river. Pass large, impressive gates for Avington Lodge. ❺ On reaching a sharp bend in the road turn left, and then turn right to pass through a kissing gate beside the drive for the golf course. Follow on the footpath straight ahead.

Continue on the grass path with a floristic strip of grasses and wild flowers on your left, and an arable field beyond. There are brambles on your right and a road beyond. Keep your dog on a lead, as the fence next to the road is low.

On reaching the end of the path pass through a kissing gate, where you will join the road. ❻ Turn left on the road and pass through the beautiful village of Avington. Continue around a bend in the road and ascend passed flint and red brick houses. After passing through the village take a road on your right which is signed for Easton and Winchester. Continue on this road, passing through a gate beside a cattle grid. You will reach the car park on your right.

18. Itchen Way

Easy - 1.9 miles - 1hr 30min

This is a lovely circular river walk, where your dog can access the water in places. The water is beautifully clear. There are also grass areas, where your dog can enjoy the freedom to run around. You will pass through some quiet roads and then walk beside a crystal clear stream, before reaching the River Itchen once again.

How to get there – The car park is situated on Garnier Road, off St. Cross Street in the centre of Winchester.

Grid Reference – SU 483280

Nearest Postcode – SO23 9PA

Parking – Free

Facilities – There are no facilities

You will need – Dog leads, dog bags

The Walk

❶ From the car park entrance, cross the road and take the footpath to your left and ahead, signed with a fingerpost for Pilgrims Trail. The River Itchen is on your left, and a large recreation field is on your right. Your dog may get access into the water a little further along.

There are mature trees, which line the path. You will reach a stock fence on your right, which will continue along the edge of the field. As the field narrows you will pass a tennis court. Put your dog on a lead here. You will then pass between a net fence on your left and houses on your right.

On reaching the end of the path turn right and pass between houses. Ascend the steps, and then turn left on an access road. Ignore a footpath on your right, and continue on the quiet road. On reaching another road, turn left. Cross the road bridge and continue on the path beside a stream.

Continue on this road beside the stream, and on reaching the end of the road take the footpath on your left. ❷ Continue on this path beside the stream on your right. You will also pass an oxbow section of the River Itchen on your left.

There is an area where your dog can access the stream on your right. You will have a field on your left. At the end of the field pass a seating area on your left, where you will now see the River Itchen once again. You will pass a private footbridge on your right. Put your dog on a lead here, as there is a road ahead.

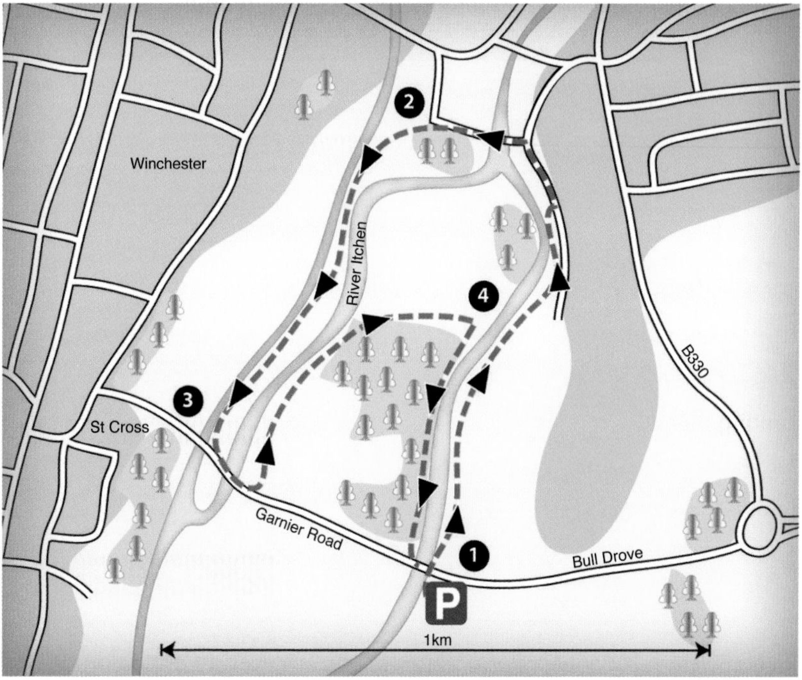

Pass beside a gate, and on reaching the road turn left. ❸ Continue beside the road for a short distance. Cross a footbridge and then turn left to enter into a playing field. Keep your dog on a lead whilst in the playing field. Keep to the edge of the playing field, following beside the fence line on your left. The river is beyond the fence.

On reaching the end of the fence, cross a footbridge over a stream and continue on the path between barbed wire fences. Trees surround the area here. Continue on the path. Cross another footbridge over the stream. The stream is now on your left. You will soon reach back beside the river.

Go through a kissing gate on your right. ❹ Keep your dog under close control as there is a sluice ahead making the water dangerous. There may also be livestock grazing. Continue on the wide grass bank with the river on your left.

Pass through another kissing gate, which is beside the sluice. Continue on the wide riverbank. When you see a gate ahead, call your dog close as you are near the road. Pass through the gate, with your dog on a short lead, and cross the road to go back into the car park.

19. St Catherine's Hill Med - 1.4 miles - 1hr 30min

This circular walk starts with an ascent through mixed broadleaved woodland. You will reach the site of St. Catherine's hill fort, where you will have stunning views of the surrounding countryside. You will walk on the perimeter of the hill fort, and then descend the hill to reach the beautiful River Itchen, where your dog will find an access spot to cool off and have a drink.

How to get there – The car park is situated on Garnier Road, off St. Cross Street in the centre of Winchester.

Grid Reference – SU 483280
Nearest Postcode – SO23 9PA

Parking – Free

Facilities – There are no facilities

You will need – Dog leads, dog bags

The Walk

❶ From the car park, at the furthest end from the road, go through the tunnel. Go through a kissing gate straight ahead. Keep your dog under close control, as there may be livestock. Ascend on the path, between the scrub and floristic grassland. On reaching a fork take the path on your left, passing beneath the trees.

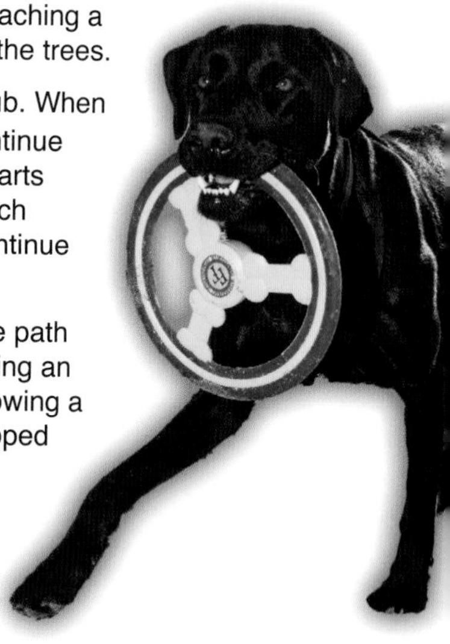

Ascend the steps with mixed grassland and scrub. When you reach the top of the hill turn left, ❷ and continue between two embankments, which are the ramparts of the ancient hill fort. Pass beneath mature beech trees. On reaching another path, cross it and continue straight ahead.

Ignore a couple of minor paths on your right. The path descends through trees and scrub and on reaching an opening turn right, on the less obvious path, following a level path on the hillside. On your left there is sloped chalk grassland and there is chalk grassland on your right, within the hill fort. Take a path on your right, which ascends onto the top of the rampart. Turn left and continue to follow the path along the rampart. There are fabulous views ahead and to your left.

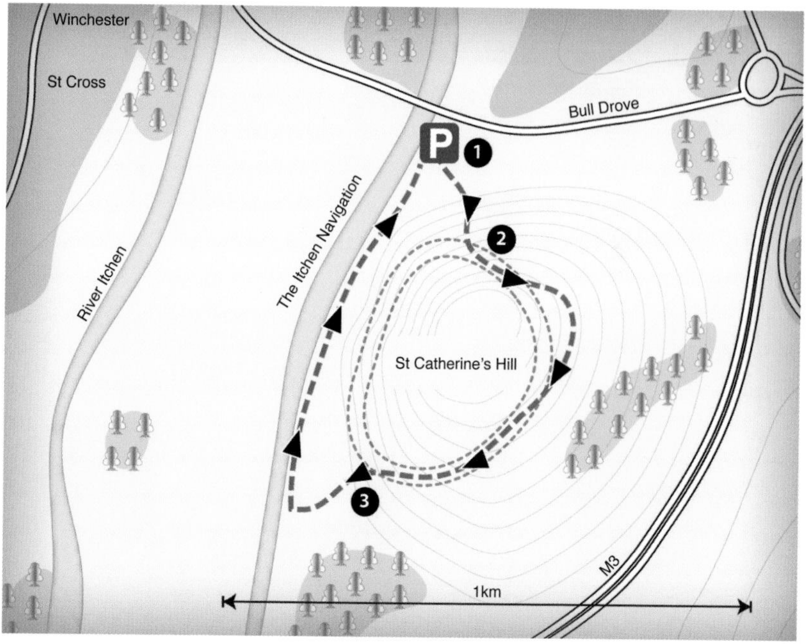

You will reach a long set of steps. ❸ Descend the steps where you will reach the bottom of the hillside. Continue on the path to a gate and pass through it. Pass beside sheep pens on your right, and pass through another gate. You will reach a tarmac path. Turn right on this path, which is shared with cyclists, so keep your dog under close control.

Continue beside the River Itchen on the wide path for a short distance. Take a narrow path on your left, where you can now walk alongside the river. Care should be taken to stop your dog getting access here as he may struggle to climb back out. This path gets narrow in places where erosion has washed away the path. There is access to the water further along. Trees line the path on your right.

You will eventually see a road bridge ahead; the car park is just before the road bridge on your right.

20. Shawford Down

Medium - 2 miles - 1hr 30min

This circular walk has many delights. There are wonderful views after a short ascent. You will walk amongst broadleaved woodland, and beautiful meadows, where in the summer months you will see many bees and butterflies. The wonderful River Itchen path offers special 'doggy dipping' areas, where your dog can cool off in the water. There may be cattle grazing at times on the common and there is a short section of road.

How to get there – From Winchester follow the sign for Southampton at first, and then follow the sign for Shawford on the B3335 St. Cross Road. Just as you reach Shawford turn right, onto the road leading to Bridge Terrace (just before going under the railway bridge). At the head of the approach road pass a car park on your right and continue, where you will reach another car park on your right.

Grid Reference – SU 471247
Postcode – SO21 2BT

Parking – Free

Facilities – There are no facilities

You will need – Dog leads, dog bags

The Walk

❶ Go to the furthest end of the car park, and with your back to the chain link fence, go over the bund straight ahead. On reaching the distinct path turn right. Continue on the grass path through the middle of the woodland ride. Take a path on your left, which leads to a set of steps. Ascend the steps into the woodland, and turn right on reaching another path.

Pass a wooden barrier and continue on the path, through a glade. On reaching back into the woods continue straight ahead. You will reach a tarmac path. Turn left here and ascend between the trees. There may be cattle grazing beyond the gate, so keep your dog under close control. The cattle are well used to dog walkers, and therefore should pay you little attention. Pass through the gate, and on reaching another path and a bench turn right.

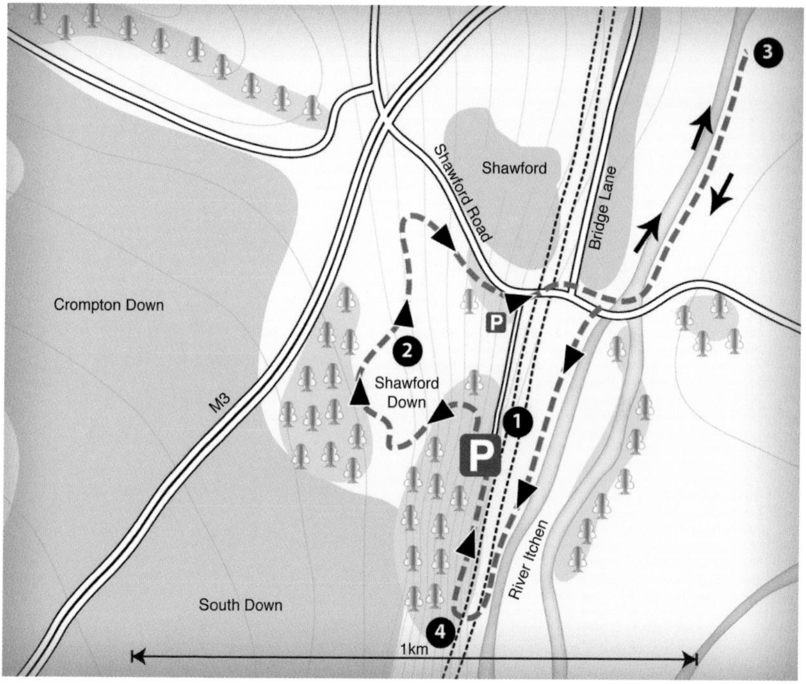

Continue on the wide grass path, through the beautiful floristic meadow. ❷ There are lovely views of the surrounding countryside on your right as you continue. Ignore paths on your left and right. Pass a stone

track on your left and a bench. Continue straight ahead, passing scrub and some trees. The path will descend and you will see houses in the distance ahead. As you turn a bend, take a path on your right before descending to the bottom of the hill.

The path cuts across the hillside. You will reach a war memorial. Pass the cross on your right and then descend the steps on your left, passing between the scrub. On reaching a grass path turn left. Take the next path on your right, which descends steeply in places to reach a gate.

Put your dog on a lead and pass through the gate. Continue straight ahead, beside a car park. Cross the quiet road, and continue straight ahead on a path between trees. Descend the steps and continue straight ahead. Pass a train station on your right and continue under the railway bridge. Pass through the village, and just before reaching the road bridge pass a footpath on your right. You have the option of extending your walk, on a liner riverside path. This is highly recommended. If you don't want to include the extension take the footpath on your right, before you cross the road bridge, and continue to section B.

A. Extended Walk. Cross the road bridge and then cross the road, to continue on the footpath straight ahead.

Follow beside the river on your left, with a garden fence on your right. Your dog can access the river after crossing a footbridge, but check the flow of the river before allowing him to enter the water. Cross the footbridge, and then your dog can get access into the river, via a specially made doggy dip. This prevents the riverbank becoming eroded from the many dogs that walk along the river. Please prevent your dog accessing the river, until you reach another doggy dip further along. The water is crystal clear and there are many aquatic plants along the way.

Gardens descend to the riverbed on the opposite side of the river. There are fields beyond the trees on your right. Continue along the river as far as you wish, but it is worth reaching the next doggy dip area, just before the sluice gate. The area here is wide, with some benches. ❸ When you turn around simply retrace your steps back to the road. Remember to put your dog on a lead as you reach the footbridge. Cross the road and turn right and then almost immediately take a path on your left.

B. Direct route. Follow the sign on the fingerpost for Itchen Navigation. Do not allow your dog to enter the river until you have accessed the river flow. Continue on the tarmac path, with the river on your left and houses on your right.

On reaching a kissing gate continue straight ahead. There is a stock fence now on your right, with a meadow beyond it. A row of trees line the river on your left. Keep your dog under close control before reaching the end of the meadow, as there is a road ahead. On reaching the road turn left. Take a path on your left, which continues beside the river. There are grasses and scrub here; keep your dog under close control, as you will return to the access road shortly. On reaching the road, cross over and pass beneath the railway tunnel. Pass through a kissing gate and turn right.

❹ Continue on the path, beside the chain link fence, at the edge of woodland. As you continue there is a clearance in the woodland, with grasses and scrub. Continue on the worn path, where you will reach the car park.

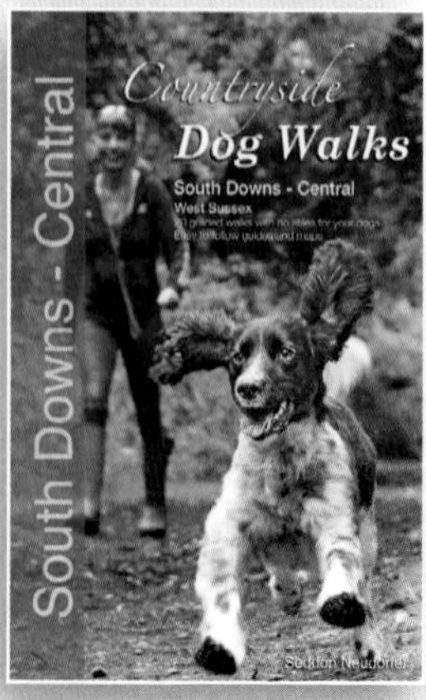

www.countrysidedogwalks.co.uk

Follow us on Facebook for progress reports on our future publications.

Search - Countryside Dog Walks

Home Made Dog Treats

Recipe Book

Seddon Neudorfer

New Release Nov - 2016

Simple recipes made from ingredients in your kitchen

Healthy ingredients to ensure a healthy dog

Fun and easy to make